MALACHI'S MESSAGE
FOR
TODAY

G. Campbell Morgan

Baker Book House   Grand Rapids, Michigan

ISBN: 0-8010-5912-7
Reprinted 1972 by
Baker Book House Company
Printed in the United States of America

Paperback edition: First printing, September 1972
Second printing, September 1974
Third printing, January 1976

Contents

I

INTRODUCTORY

I

INTRODUCTORY

IN order that we may approach the study of this book intelligently, it is necessary that certain principles of interpretation should be recognized and accepted. To the statement and consideration of these principles this introductory chapter is devoted.

I

Read first in Paul's letters to the Romans, xv. 4: "For whatsoever things were written aforetime were written for our learning, that we through patience and comfort of the Scriptures might have hope." If we consider that verse in its setting we shall find that Paul, having made a quotation from the Old Testament Scriptures, interpolates upon the general scheme of his argument, a declaration that the inspired writing of Scripture does not exhaust itself in that particular age to which it is addressed. That is one of the peculiar notes of inspiration. Inspired writings differ from all others, in that they are not produced for one age exclusively, but have perpetually a varying application to varying ages.

11

The finest literature the world has produced, apart from the literature of the Bible, while it will remain interesting for long years—even though the conditions of the age to which it appealed may have changed—will not have a living and practical application to any age save that in which it was penned. The writings of Chaucer are of absorbing interest to Englishmen to-day, because they reveal to us the age in which they were produced, but they have no vital message to the men of to-day.

In that particular, this whole Book of God is in entire contrast to all other writings. All Scripture " written aforetime " had a local application, and a distinctive message to the times in which it was written, but it was written also " for our learning."

The apostle, in this verse, makes use of the word " Scriptures "—" that we through patience and comfort of the Scriptures might have hope." This word occurs in the New Testament no less than fifty-one times; and, with only one exception, is used in reference to the recognized Scriptures of the people of Israel, known to us as the Old Testament. It may be well for us to turn to that one exception, because it will enable us to keep that fact in mind. 2 Peter iii. 16 : " As also in all his epistles, speaking in them of these things ; in which are some things hard to be understood, which

they that are unlearned and unstable wrest, as
they do also the other Scriptures, unto their
own destruction."

It is probable that when Peter makes use of
the phrase "other Scriptures," he may be re-
ferring principally to New Testament writings
which are beginning to be scattered. It is not
an established fact. He may have referred in
this case, as in every other, to the Old Testa
ment, but there is a probability that he is
making reference to New Testament writings
—to those letters that are being distributed to
the Church of Jesus Christ. That is the only
case in the New Testament where it is at all
possible to read into the expression "Scriptures" that interpretation. In every other
case the term refers to the recognized Scriptures of the Jewish people; and in that fact
we discover that the New Testament has put
its decided seal upon the Old. You cannot
say, "I take the New and not the Old." If
you accept the New, the Old is interwoven
into every book that the New contains.

In this connection I would suggest a pro-
foundly interesting experiment to Bible stu-
dents, which, while it is an experiment, is nevertheless profitable. Take your New Testament, and for once read it through from a lit-
erary standpoint, with the object of finding
out how many chapters there are in which

there is no quotation from, and no allusion to, the Old, and see how much you have left.

Here then is a principle that we must keep in memory—what was "written aforetime" was written not only with a direct bearing upon the time, but "for our learning." In other words, when the Holy Spirit of God moved men of old to write, He not only moved them to write with a view to the interests of the times in which they lived, but with a view to all who should come after them.

II

Let us now turn to one of the most important of the Old Testament Scriptures, Deuteronomy vi. 1–4, "Now these are the commandments, the statutes, and the judgments, which the Lord your God commanded to teach you, that ye might do them in the land whither ye go to possess it : That thou mightest fear the Lord thy God, to keep all His statutes and His commandments, which I command thee, thou, and thy son, and thy son's son, all the days of thy life ; and that thy days may be prolonged. Hear therefore, O Israel, and observe to do it ; that it may be well with thee, and that ye may increase mightily, as the Lord God of thy fathers hath promised thee, in the land that floweth with milk and honey. Hear, O Israel : The Lord our God is one Lord." Among the things " written aforetime " is to be found this statement of a great principle underlying all life. The whole economy of Divine Government gathers round that verse: " Hear, O Israel: the Lord our God is one Lord." That was the special truth that was committed to the nation of Israel to preserve as a sacred thing, amid the nations of the earth. It is the central truth of all Divine Government and of all human life: " God is one."

Mathematics is spoken of as being an exact science. Is it exact? I think not. Nothing is absolutely proved. That two and two make four, no one can prove. It never has been proved, and it is quite impossible to prove it— that is, you cannot demonstrate the truth of it.

Euclid is exact surely; it is built up step by step; you cannot do Book II., until you have done Book I. Come back to the early days of school life, and every boy knows he cannot do his " Pons Asinorum " without knowing the first proposition. It must then be exact. Let us examine it. How is it built up? Unless you learn your definitions, and believe in them, you cannot do Euclid. What are your definitions? " A point is position without magnitude." Absolutely absurd! You cannot have position without magnitude. The instant you admit position you admit magnitude. " A line

is length without breadth." Equally absurd!
You cannot have one without the other.

So our exact things are built up on impossi-
bilities and absurd positions. All mathematical science may be reduced to a common fact.
What is that common fact? *One!* When
you have said "one" you have said "two,"
and when you have said a "million" you have
said "one." You cannot get beyond "one."
One is essential, two is accidental.

"The Lord your God is one Lord." God is
behind everything the final certain *One.* You
cannot analyze, or divide, or explain Him, yet
He is the one and only absolute certainty.
He is ONE, all-comprehending, indivisible.
When you have said that, you have said all.
When you have omitted that, you have left
everything out, and babbled only in chaotic
confusion.

From that truth I make a deduction. If
God is *one*, then the principles and the purposes of His government never vary. Dispensations and methods change; the will of God
never changes, never varies, never progresses,
in that sense. What does progress mean?
Failure! What does advancement mean?
Past limitations! You cannot progress unless
there has been failure somewhere. If I can
be better in five minutes than I am now, I am
wrong now. Progress is a confession of fail-

ure. When this age boasts of its vaunted progress, it is telling the story of the failure of the past. God never makes progress, never advances. Consequently He is not always doing as we are, legislating for man—framing new laws because the old ones have failed. The will of right, love, and tenderness, *His* will is eternal.

Dispensations come and go, dawn and vanish; but God remains the same, underneath, with, and in each. Some people speak as though God had not only altered His methods, but His mind. I agree that He has changed His methods, but His mind, never! God did not begin to love man when Jesus came. Jesus came to roll back the curtain and show man the heart that was eternal, the love that was always there. Christianity is not God's alteration of attitude toward man. It is not that in the old dispensation He was a policeman, and in this a father. He has always been a father, He never changes.

Dispensations and methods mark the change of man, and the necessary change in the way the Divine Hand is placed upon human life, but behind everything—God!

> God the same abiding,
>   His praise shall tune my voice,
> And while in Him confiding
>   I cannot but rejoice.

We must get our feet down upon this abiding rock. It is for this reason that the Old Testament Scriptures are of value. The accidents of human life perpetually change; the essentials abide forever.

III

If we accept these principles we can now move forward another step. The prophetic messages are preëminently suited, as it seems to me, to the age in which we live, and there is a sense in which they are of more value today than even the writings of the apostles.

I do not undervalue these apostolic writings, but there are reasons why the prophetic utterances come with greater force.

The apostolic writings are expositions of God's new application of eternal truth in a new dispensation. With Jesus, the new dispensation dawned, a fresh light broke upon the senses of man. New methods came into operation. The Eternal God is the same, but fresh light from the essential light of Deity broke forth, and the apostles under inspiration—inspiration which grew out of local requirements—wrote their definition of that new light. To us, their writings are the prisms which divide the essential light into its component parts and glories. And so I read the apostolic writings, and I have my theology.

They are most valuable, we can never do without them.

The prophetic writings are not expositions of truth in that sense at all. They are almost invariably addressed to people who know truth as enshrined in their own dispensation, and they are messages to call these people to be obedient thereto.

In that sense the prophetic writings come to us with a force that the apostolic writings do not possess. We know the truth of God as no other age has ever known it, and yet there never was a time when men, knowing and living under its blessings, were less obedient to it than now. So then the " Scriptures written aforetime for our learning " demand our attention, and will always repay solemn searching, and prayerful inquiry as to their deep and inner meaning. Such are the principles upon which we base our study.

IV

Now as to the times of the book of Malachi and its author. It is almost universally admitted—indeed, one may say that it is so far admitted that there remains no doubt or question about it—that the book occupies its right place in the arrangement of the Old Testament Scriptures, that Malachi himself was the last of the Old Testament prophets.

There can be little doubt further, that the message is closely associated with the work of Nehemiah, and if Malachi is to be read intelligently, Nehemiah should be read at the same time. Malachi bears a Divine message to the condition of things portrayed in the history of Nehemiah. The proofs of this are largely and mostly to be found in the books themselves. Let us turn to only three coincidences.

i. Nehemiah xiii. 29 : " Remember them, O my God, because they have defiled the priesthood, and the covenant of the priesthood, and of the Levites." Remembering the force of these words, turn to the prophecy of Malachi ii. 8 : " But ye are departed out of the way ; ye have caused many to stumble at the law ; ye have corrupted the covenant of Levi, saith the Lord of Hosts." Nehemiah complains in the closing years of his history that the priesthood has corrupted the covenant; while Malachi, in this second chapter, addresses himself very largely to the priests, and the specific charge that he brings against them is that they have corrupted the covenant of Levi. It is a peculiar expression which we shall consider more closely when we come to study the book itself.

ii. In that same chapter of Nehemiah (reading from the twenty-third verse to the twenty-seventh) you find that Nehemiah complains

that the peculiar people of God have entered
into unholy alliance with idolaters in the way
of marriage, and follows that complaint by
separating those thus united. Malachi speaks
of exactly the same condition of things in the
second chapter (verses ten to sixteen), the evil
of mixed marriages, and the awful neglect
which ends in the tears and sobs of the women
about the altars of God.

iii. Again, in the last chapter of Nehemiah
and the tenth verse: "I perceived that the
portions of the Levites had not been given
them: for the Levites and the singers, that
did the work, were fled every one to his field."
Malachi iii. 10 calls attention to this omission,
saying, "Bring ye all the tithes into the storehouse, that there may be meat in Mine house,
and prove Me now herewith, saith the Lord of
Hosts, if I will not open you the windows of
heaven." These three notes establish the fact
that Malachi's prophecy was uttered in the
days of Nehemiah's influence. I do not say in
the days of Nehemiah. I know that it is a remarkable thing, upon which comment has not
been wanting, that Malachi's name does not
appear either in the book of Ezra or Nehemiah.
It seems most probable that Malachi's name is
not mentioned because he follows immediately
after Nehemiah. The people have fallen back
into the very abuses that Nehemiah set him-

self to rectify, and Malachi is raised up, the last of the prophets, to bear this message to them.

Nothing whatever is known of the nationality or parentage of Malachi. The name itself is a significant one, and there have been those who have read the name simply as a title—"My messenger." Others say that Malachi was an incarnation of an angelic messenger. I do not accept either of these theories. I believe the man's name was Malachi. The Septuagint gives it as Malachius, and so most likely Malachi is an abbreviated form of Malachia. It means "the messenger of Jehovah," but if, because it has that peculiar meaning, we argue it is merely a title, let it be remembered, Joel means "the Lord Jehovah."

But while that is so, it is noticeable that he was exceedingly careful to speak of himself only as "a bearer of the burden of the word of God." He says nothing of himself. You cannot read this prophecy without seeing how he has excluded himself from it. You read Amos, and right through, you discover his calling in the figures he uses. The man lives in it, very beautifully, but in this case the Lord's messenger is absolutely hidden behind the message he comes to bring. There is nothing from which we can gather his past history or trace anything concerning him. He is simply Malachi, the messenger, he comes to bear the message, and the burden of the word of the Lord is so upon him, and so consumes him, that we never hear a whisper of his own personality, or catch the faintest glimpse of himself.

The peculiar need of the age in which he spoke and wrote was a distinct and direct message, and it was that distinct and direct message from God that he came to pronounce. In that fact I find one of the strongest arguments for the application of that message to this age. We need more than anything else to-day, that our preachers should be messengers of God, that the people should be spoken to, as out of the divine oracles; not that the preacher is to be an oracle, for that would be a return to the worst form of priestism, but that he is to be a messenger, and that even the fact of his being a messenger is to be lost sight of in the enormous weight of the message he comes to proclaim.

Standing upon these rock foundations, we come to the consideration of truths that are fresh as the Spring; new, as God is new, and not simply to delve among parchments and musty history.

II

THE SPIRIT OF THE AGE

II

THE SPIRIT OF THE AGE

I

WE come now to the consideration of the condition of the people at the time when Malachi uttered his prophecy. There is a key-word in the book revealing this condition, a word these people used in reply to every message which the prophet delivered to them, showing what their real attitude was. It is the word "Wherein." Let us consider the seven occasions of its use :—

(1) Chap. i., ver. 2.—"I have loved you, saith the Lord. Yet ye say, *Wherein* hast Thou loved us?"

(2) Chap. i., ver. 6.—"A son honoreth his father, and a servant his master: if then I be a Father, where is Mine honor? and if I be a Master, where is My fear? saith the Lord of Hosts unto you, O priests, that despise My name. And ye say, *Wherein* have we despised Thy name?"

(3) Chap. i., ver. 7.—"Ye offer polluted bread upon Mine altar. And ye say, *Wherein* have we polluted Thee?"

(4) Chap. ii., ver. 17.—" Ye have wearied the Lord with your words. Yet ye say, *Wherein* have we wearied Him ? "

(5) Chap. iii., ver. 7.—" Return unto Me, and I will return unto you, saith the Lord of Hosts. But ye said, *Wherein* shall we return ? "

(6) Chap. iii., ver. 8.—" Will a man rob God ? Yet ye have robbed Me. But ye say, *Wherein* have we robbed Thee ? "

(7) Chap. iii., ver. 13.—" Your words have been stout against Me, saith the Lord. Yet ye say, *Wherein* have we spoken so much against Thee ? "

You notice in this last instance the authorized version gives the word " What," which is a peculiar accident of translation. It is the same word in the Hebrew, and ought to have been translated " Wherein," as in the other cases.

Thus we have this word, " Wherein," put by the prophet into the mouth of those people seven distinct times, with reference to seven distinct announcements. He comes to them first of all with the declaration: " I have loved you, saith the Lord," and they say, " *Wherein* hast Thou loved us ? " Then he says, " Ye have despised the Lord," and they say, " *Wherein* have we despised Him ? " And then: " Ye have polluted My altar," and they

say, " *Wherein* have we polluted Thine altar ? "
And then :   " Ye have wearied Me," and they
say, " *Wherein* have we wearied Thee ? "   And
then :   " Return   to   Me,"   and   they   say,
" *Wherein*   shall   we   return ? "   And   then :
" Ye have robbed Me," and they say, " *Wherein*
have we robbed Thee ? "   And lastly :   " Ye
have   spoken   against   Me,"   and   they   say,
" *Wherein* have we spoken against Thee ? "

This   word   shows   us   the   condition of these
people in a lurid light.   The temple is rebuilt,
the altar is set up, the sacrifices are offered, the
feasts and fasts are alike observed, and to these
people—with outward form and ritual, perfect
to   the   very   last   and   minutest   detail—the
prophecy comes, the Divine complaint is made.
And   they   look   at   the   prophet   with   mingled
astonishment and incredulity, and they say,
" Wherein ?   What do you mean ?   You charge
us with having despised God and polluted His
altar, with having wearied Him, and with wandering from and refusing to return to Him, and
accuse   us   of   robbing   and   speaking   against
Him ; we don't see that we have done these
things, so why should we be subjected to these
accusations ?   You come and say we despise
God's work.   Look at our sacrifices and offerings !   You tell us that we have polluted the
altar.   We have brought our gifts !   You tell
us that we have wearied Him.   We don't see

where or when! We are not conscious of having done anything to displease Him! You tell us to return. We don't see where we are to return from; we don't see where we are to return to! You tell us we have robbed God. We want to know when? You say we have spoken against God. We don't remember having spoken against Him; when was it?" '

What is the significance of this word "Wherein?" These people are not in open rebellion against God, nor do they deny His right to offerings, but they are laboring under the delusion, that because they have brought offerings, they have been true to Him all along. Theirs is not the language of a people throwing off a yoke and saying, "We will not be loyal," but of a people established in the temple. It is not the language of a people who say, "Let us cease to sacrifice, and worship; and let us do as we please"; but it is the language of a people who say, "We are sacrificing and worshipping to please God," and yet He says, by the mouth of His servant, "Ye have wearied Me: ye have robbed and spoken against Me."

They have been most particular and strict in outward observances, but their hearts have been far away from their ceremonials. They have been boasting themselves in their knowledge of truth, responding to that knowledge

mechanically, technically; but their hearts,
their lives, their characters, the inwardness of
their natures, have been a perpetual contradiction in the eye of Heaven, to the will of
God; and, when the prophet tells them what
God thinks of them, they, with astonishment
and impertinence, look into his face and say,
"We don't see this at all!" To translate it
into the language of the New Testament—
"having the form of godliness, they deny the
power." They have passed into the fearful
condition of imagining that what God asks for
is but the letter, and they are failing to understand that the letter is, at best, but an awkward representation of what God is demand-
ing in the spirit.

I say "awkward," simply because the letter
never can convey all the spiritual meanings.
When a man is willing to obey the letter with
spiritual intent, then God has more to say than
the letter can contain. These people have
come simply to bear a literal yoke. They are
the most orthodox people, and yet their whole
heart is outside the matter, and the facts of
their lives are hidden, alas! from themselves,
so subtle and awful in the influence of getting
away from direct and close dealing with God.
I say these facts are hidden from their own
eyes. They are not conscious of it, but God is
changed to their conception. The God of

their fathers is not their God. The God of spiritual communion with His people, who walked and talked with the patriarchs, is not their God. The god of Israel in the days of Malachi, the god whom they had invented, and were trying to appease and worship, was the god of trivialities, of mechanical observances, the god who asks for a temple with a set number of stones and corners, the altar of such a shape, and so many sacrifices and prayers, without any reference to character. When the prophet came to these people, he came to a people who were feeling thoroughly satisfied with their religious observances, and were prepared to say, " Wherein have we done this, or failed to do that ? "

II

Now let us go further to discover the reason of their condition. The second chapter begins with these words : " And now, O ye priests, this commandment is for you ; " and the seventh verse reads : " For the priest's lips should keep knowledge, and they should seek the law at his mouth : for he is the messenger of the Lord of Hosts." That is the Divine conception of the priesthood. The priest should not only have the knowledge, but should keep it, that is, walk in it, be obedient to it, be the embodiment of the knowledge he holds, of

which he is the depositary for the time being.
The people "should seek the law at his mouth,"
for he is the messenger of the Lord of Hosts.
More, he is to tell them the will of God, and
that not simply as one who possesses it as a
wonderful theory, but as one who is himself
living within the realm thereof.

That is the ideal. What then has the
prophet to say to the priests? (ii. 8): "Ye are
departed out of the way; ye have caused
many to stumble at the law; ye have corrupted the covenant of Levi, saith the Lord of
Hosts." Now all this teaches us, that at the
back of the declension of the people is the declension and corruption of the priest; that the
people failed to have a right conception of
God, because the priest ceased to give them
the true conception. The whole company of
the people have passed out of the high spiritual realm of past history, because the priest
has tampered with—corrupted as the word is
here—the very covenant of God.

In reading Nehemiah in connection with
Malachi, you will have noticed something to
which I shall ask you to refer for a moment.
Nehemiah xiii. 28, 29: "And one of the sons
of Joiada, the son of Eliashib, the high priest,
was son-in-law to Sanballat the Horonite:
therefore I chased him from me. Remember
them, O my God, because they have defiled

the priesthood, and the covenant of the priesthood and of the Levites." There you have an
example, a historic statement of this very
thing, the case of a priest marrying the daughter of Sanballat the Horonite.

Read the history of Nehemiah and see how
much Sanballat was, or was not, in accord
with the purpose of God. Sanballat was the
embodiment of the spirit that was antagonistic
to the Word and Spirit of God. One of the
priests of God has married his daughter, and
Nehemiah says with that magnificent vehe-
mence which characterized all his splendid
work: "I chased him from me." Why did
you do it, Nehemiah? Why did you chase
him away? "Because he had defiled the
priesthood, by defiling the covenant of the
priesthood and the Levites." The same word
occurs in Malachi: "Ye are departed out of
the way; ye have caused many to stumble at
the law; ye have corrupted the covenant of
Levi, saith the Lord of Hosts." The priesthood,
instead of keeping the law, had "departed out
of the way." The priests had announced the
law, they had read its articles, they had pro-
claimed it as law, and then had debased it
themselves. Corruption had come into the
covenant by the way of the priesthood.

What was the priesthood for? The only
reason for its existence was that there should

be on the human side a guarding of the articles of the covenant of God, and no man who himself corrupts, tampers with, breaks the covenant, can for a single moment, by his teaching, uphold it; and the trouble at the back of the national declension was the declension of the priesthood. The teachers of the people, the messengers of God, had themselves done despite to the law of God, by proclaiming it as fact, and denying it in their own lives.

This then was the spirit of the age. Formalism, ritual, ceremonial—everything so far as mechanical and outward observance—complete. A Divine messenger came voicing the complaint of God, and the people in astonishment and anger, and with marked impertinence, looked into the very face of high heaven and said, "We don't see this thing at all—Wherein?" And all this because God's appointed messengers have themselves, in life, and work, and conversation corrupted the covenant, and have passed into the region of baseness and contempt in the eyes of the people.

III

There is, I fear, an awful sense in which that picture is a picture of the age in which we live. Never was there a day when organ-

izations were more complete, and outward
and mechanical forms of service more numer-
ous than they are now, but I am not going to
dwell merely upon ritual.

I have made reference to a verse with which
you are all familiar—2 Timothy iii. 1–4:
" This know also, that in the last days perilous
times shall come. For men shall be lovers of
their ownselves, covetous, boasters, proud,
blasphemers, disobedient to parents, unthank-
ful, unholy. Without natural affection, truce-
breakers, false accusers, incontinent, fierce,
despisers of those that are good. Traitors,
heady, high-minded, lovers of pleasures more
than lovers of God." I ask you very solemnly
to read that description and apply it to the
age in which we live.

Take the next verse, five, for it is that to which
I wish to come: " Having a form of godliness,
but denying the power thereof." Will you—
bearing that verse in mind—turn to Paul's
letter to the Romans (second chapter and the
twentieth verse), and very patiently follow the
thought? You must go back for a moment to the
seventeenth verse in order to catch the meaning
of his words: " Thou art called a Jew—an in-
structor of the foolish, a teacher of babes,
which hast the *form* of knowledge and of the
truth in the law." I have read that passage in
order that we may bring these two words

together. In the twentieth verse of the second
chapter of Romans and in the fifth verse of
the third chapter of second Timothy you have
the same word "form." These are the only
two occasions where that actual word occurs
in the whole of the New Testament. Of
course, you get the word "form" translated
from other words, but this word is μορφωσις,
and it means "formation" rather than "form."
It refers to the possibility of a process rather
than to a thing accomplished. When Paul
said to Timothy that in these last days perilous
times should come, that men would have the
form of godliness and yet deny the power
he marked a danger more subtle than that of
ritualism. It means that in the last days men
will actually come to possess the truth itself
which is the formative power of godliness, and
yet will deny the power. A man may have
the very formation of godliness, he may hold
the truth, he may be the most orthodox man
in the whole city, and yet deny the power.

That is one of the dangers of the present
day. Take Christendom at large. You have
thousands of people who can give you good
reasons for belonging to the Church, who have
some purity in their lives responding to the
claims of Jesus Christ, and seem to be not only
maintaining the outward forms, but appear
also to hold tenaciously to the truth which is

the formative power of the Church, and yet whose lives are not in correspondence to the truth they hold.

In this sense there is an element of danger in our great conventions. Do not misunderstand me. I am not undervaluing them. I thank God for the blessed work being accomplished through them, but there are men and women who are able to enunciate the whole scheme, not only of regeneration but also of sanctification, and yet in their actual life,— when lifted away from the crowd of their fellow Christians, and from the opinion of their fellow men, into the white light of Divine requirement, which alone reveals character,—it can be said of them "denying the power."

Tell such men it is not a new extension scheme, not a discussion of this constitution or that, we need, but a red-hot fire purging out the dross, and they say "Wherein? Have we not all these things? Do we not hold the truth? Are we not orthodox?—Wherein?"

What is at the back of all this? As in the old days, so now, there has been a corrupting of the priesthood, there has been a corrupting of the covenant by the teachers, who ought to have led us into the deep things of God.

What is God's covenant? If you read the eighth chapter of Hebrews in connection with the thirty-first chapter of Jeremiah, beginning

with the thirty-first verse and reading on, you
will find that the covenant of God with His
people, for this dispensation, is in advance of
the old covenant. That was a covenant in
which God was married to His people, and
they were to be kept by outward laws, words
written upon tables of stone, commandments
uttered in their hearing, and the marriage relationship was to be maintained between the
chosen people and God, in that covenant, by
obedience to those laws.

What is the new covenant? The new covenant is, "I will write my law upon your heart
and upon your mind," and the relation of people in the new covenant to God is to be the
relation of a new birth, of an actual affinity,
of a marvellous identification. I am no longer
married to God in the sense of maintaining the
relation by obedience to an outward rule of
life, but in the union of a child of God, born
again in His Spirit; with His law, not given
to me from the outside, but written on my
mind and on my heart.

Is that covenant corrupted, nay, is not Christendom corrupted from end to end? If a man
begin to talk about inward cleansing, about
the necessity for the fire-blood cleansing of
the nature, before men can live in communion
with God, how many there are who say at
once, "We are talking of things that are im-

possible." So long as we who teach corrupt
the covenant by going back to Judaism, by
lowering the high and awful requirement of
actual new birth and spiritual affinity, just so
long will the people be content with holding
a form of truth and denying the power.

There is then an awful application of Malachi's days and the spirit of his age to this age
and to these days. There was a lowering of
the standard of the Divine requirement by the
priest—using that word in the Divine sense of
the messenger of God—and the people boasting too often in their correct theory of worship,
super-orthodox, were yet, in their inner life, in
the depth of their own nature, in the actual
fact of what God alone knows, " denying the
power."

Let us go alone into His presence, for that
is light, and fire, and life, and ceasing to be
content with conventional religion let each
one for himself and herself, in that awful
Presence say, " O God, save me from mere
correctness of view, and that curiosity to
know, for the sake of knowing only, which
has blighted my life, and make me what Thou
wouldst have me to be in actual character."

III

THE COMPLAINTS OF JEHOVAH

THE COMPLAINTS OF JEHOVAH

AGAINST this people—formal and self-satisfied—God, by the mouth of His messenger, uttered seven complaints which may thus be summarized: Profanity, Sacrilege, Greed, Weariness in service, Honoring of vice—or Treason against the covenant of Heaven—Robbery from God, and Blasphemy against Him. To these complaints they responded with the question " Wherein ? " There is a profanity far worse than that of the slum; a sacrilege far more terrible than the act of breaking into the sacred place and purloining the vessels of the sanctuary ; a greed which is more atrocious than the greed of a man who professes no godliness, but openly worships Mammon; a weariness in service which even exceeds in wickedness an entire abstention from service; a form of treason by the honoring of vice, which is more awful than outward and open plotting—however diabolic it may be—to dethrone God; a kind of robbery which is more terrible than the actual abstraction of coins from the treasury of the Most High; a kind of blasphemy that in comparison makes the revolting blasphemy of the streets seem almost insignificant and obtuse.

I

In proceeding to consider the first—Profanity, turn to the first chapter of the prophecy, and read the sixth and seventh verses: " A son honoreth his father, and a servant his master: if then I be a Father, where is Mine honor ? and if I be a Master, where is My fear ? " Now pass to the seventh verse : " Ye offer polluted bread upon Mine altar "—and the last sentence of the verse—" in that," that is to say, in the offering of the polluted bread, " in that ye say, the table of the Lord is contemptible."

Here we find the people calling God, " Father," and yet giving Him no honor; calling Him " Master," and having no fear of Him; saying the table is contemptible by placing upon that table polluted bread; and yet they say " Wherein ? " that is, they are perfectly satisfied that God is their Father, they are perfectly orthodox in that matter, they will not for a moment dispute with any one the fact that God is their Master, but fight for the position when any one dares to traverse it. Yet God comes and says : " Ye call Me Father, and ye call Me Master : where is My honor, and where is My fear ? "

They bring their bread to the altar, and, I think that if you had had the opportunity of examining it, you would not have found it polluted in the ordinary, literal sense of the word. With a surprised inflection in your voice you would have said, "That bread is not polluted!" Yet it was polluted, by the hands of the very men who placed it there. What is profanity? The root meaning of the word is "away from the temple" (*pro*, from; *fanum*, temple), and it has come to be used with reference to things not sacred, but commonplace.

These people were guilty of profanity in the worst possible way, in that they took the names of God, and claimed the relationship that those names imply: Father, "honor"; Master, "fear"; and yet they did not fear Him; they accorded Him no honor save in their words, and their creeds, and their outward doings. Thus they degraded the sacred things of God to the common level of mediocrity, and in effect made the statement, "The table is contemptible."

No polluted man can offer pure bread upon God's altar; in taking or rejecting gifts He measures them by the character of the man who brings them. Let us take an illustration. It has often been asked why Abel's gift was accepted and Cain's refused. Sometimes we

have been told because Abel brought a lamb
and Cain fruit. The true reason was that
Abel was righteous and Cain was unrighteous.
Both of these men brought of the first-fruits of
their own labor, and peculiar calling in life.
I know there is another side to the subject, and
one full of interest, that the very righteousness of Abel had spoken to him of his need of
sacrifice, and therefore he was prompted to
offer a lamb; but Cain's gift was refused because Cain was refused, and Abel's gift was
accepted because Abel was accepted. In this
case, men approached the table and laid their
gifts upon it, saying " Father," and " Master ";
but before they came to that table there had
been no " honor " for the " Father," no " fear "
for the " Master." They themselves were not
accepted, and their gifts, therefore, were refused.

Profanity at its worst is to be found in the
place of outward service, in the very taber-
nacles of the Most High. To-day, it is the
profanity of Christendom. I do not say the
profanity of the Church: the Church and
Christendom are two things. Christendom is
the outward profession of Christianity, which
has libelled Christ, and driven the mass of the
people away from our services and our ordi-
nances. There is no profanity which is so
awful as that of orthodox expression and

heterodox heart. Gifts presented to God by hands that are impure, are themselves impure, for God only receives the gift according as He has received the giver. The offering that we bring to God is the true expression of the value at which we appraise the altar. If a man says, "I honor the altar of God," and then puts upon it something that his own life has contaminated, his true estimate of the value of the altar is not the statement he vouchsafes, but his contaminated gift. Such a consideration should make us exceedingly careful how we give to God, and save us from that heresy of heresies, of imagining that we can purchase our acceptance by our gifts. God receives or rejects all the gifts of man in proportion as He has received or rejected the giver.

If that be a true statement, how many gifts are not received by God which have been placed upon His altar? And is not this profanity within Christendom to-day more terribly profane and far-reaching in its evil influence than all the profanity of the slum?

II

The second of these complaints is to be found in the eighth verse of the same chapter: "And if ye offer the blind for sacrifice, is it not evil? and if ye offer the lame and the

sick, is it not evil? offer it now unto thy
Governor; will he be pleased with thee, or
accept thy person? saith the Lord of Hosts."
Here is a movement forward in evil, something beyond profanity, viz, sacrilege; the
sin which grows out of profanity, as surely as
the sin of profanity is committed. These men
are now absolutely offering to God the blind,
and the lame, and the sick. The Divine requirement under the Mosaic economy was that
"the lamb placed upon the altar should be
without spot or blemish—the finest of the
flock," but these men have lost the sense of
what worship means, in that they have retained the finest of the flock for themselves,
and brought to the altar that which engen-
ders its contempt, simply to keep up the
form of sacrifice and the appearance which
they so much covet. God calls them to account for this display of meanness, and He
says—mark the poignant sarcasm of the
prophet's words—" offer it to your Governor,
the man who rules over you, the kind of offering you are putting upon Mine altar—will he
accept it ? "

Why this complaint ?   Because the offerings
put upon the altar were valueless to the men
who placed them there, and God always values the offering by what it cost the man who
brings it, and never by its intrinsic worth.

Have we learned that lesson even to-day ; a
lesson which the Master emphasized when He
sat and watched the people of His own time—
the direct descendants of these men of Malachi—putting their offerings into the treasury ?
He did not measure a single gift, intrinsically ;
but by its cost to the soul who offered it.   The
rich men gave of their abundance. He saw
every gift, recognized its worth, was cognizant
of its marketable value, in every case.   Pres-
ently there came along a woman who was a
widow, and she dropped in two mites.   Listen
to the Master of the treasury,—the One to
whom the gifts are brought.   What did He
say ?   " That woman has done well " ?   He
said something far more sweeping than that.
Did He say, " She has cast in more than any
man " ?   No ! but " *More than they all.* "   In
effect, He said, " Bring all the gifts that have
fallen into the treasury to-day, and put them
together, and these mites outweigh them all in
the balances of God."

He measured the gift then, as ever, by its
cost to the giver.   The men who had put into
the treasury out of their abundance did not
forego any luxury when they reached home.
There was no self-denial in their giving, and
each might have said, as men often say to-day,
" I do not miss what I give."   To such, let me
say, God does not thank you for your gift.

The widow sadly missed her two mites. They meant a meal, and the only meal in view, and because her gift was sacrificial, God accepted and prized it infinitely more than any other. What does sacrifice reveal? Not a selfish seeking for favor, but a soul's estimate of the One to whom the gift is offered.

Sacrilege we have always thought was the breaking into a church and stealing therefrom. That is not so; *it is going into Church and putting something on the plate.* Do not forget that. Sacrilege is centered in offering God something which costs nothing, because you think God is worth nothing. God looks for the giving at His altar of a gift that costs something.

Men are perpetually bringing into the Christian Church the things they do not need themselves. I know there is much sacrificial giving, thank God, but there is also an enormous amount of sacrilegious giving abroad in the world to-day, giving devoid of sacrifice. We offer to God in the Church, things which we would never offer to our governors. This is sacrilege. If the giving in the Church of God to-day was of the type and the pattern of the gift of the widow to the treasury in the days long since passed away, the work of God would never have to go begging to men and women outside the Church.

III

In the tenth verse, God asks the people: "Who is there even among you that would shut the doors for nought? neither do ye kindle fire on Mine altar for nought."[1] This is the most awful indictment of greed to be found in the book. These people were opening His doors and kindling fires, because they anticipated gain thereby. There was an ulterior motive in every gift placed upon the altar, and in every deed performed, and service rendered. The service of God had degenerated into the slavery of a selfish interest; men "opened doors and kindled fires" in order that they might secure a reward. This utterance is in the form of a question and in that form only shall I make any application of it to the age in which we live. "Who is there among you that would shut the doors for nought?" Why do we render God service?—and I am going to take the highest point of view which

[1] The majority of Modern Commentators in common with the revised version agree in translating the Hebrew word *chinnâm*, "in vain." This word occurs thirty-two times in the Old Testament, and out of that number is translated six times "for nought" in the Authorized. *Five of these the Revised retains,* and only here makes the alteration. The root idea of the word is "without a cause," and so it is translated fifteen times. I have deliberately followed the example of Dr. Pusey and retained the older translation as being more in harmony with the word in its original meaning, and with the general spirit of the context as I understand it.

is also the most solemn—because we hope for
reward in the future? If so, we are treading
dangerously near this most awful manifesta-
tion of greed.

God wants men who will render service to
Him for the very love of Him, even though
they never have reward. You remember
Job's great word : "Though He slay me, yet
will I trust Him." How often is that passage
erroneously quoted, as though Job meant to
say, " If He slay me, it will be all right ; there
is something beyond it, I shall not lose everything." That is not the true interpretation.
The word " slay " goes to the deepest fact of
his being, and he intended to say, " Though He
slay me "—not " Though He permit me to be
slain by my enemies "—but, " Though I have
no future, and never see Him on His throne,
though He blot me out, yet I trust Him."
That is magnificent trust, and goes far beyond
the trust that hopes for reward.

Of course this is much higher ground than
that intended in Malachi's days, but then we
are living in a much higher dispensation. Is
our service Divine or human? When we give
the cup of cold water, if we give it for the
sake of reward we do not give it at all. When
we minister to men who are sick and in prison,
if we do it in order that He may give us His
word in days to come we do not minister at

all. God is asking for that abandonment of
man to Himself which says, "We pour all at
Thy feet, and if Thou shouldst crown us, we
would rejoice, but only that a crown was ours
to cast at the feet of Christ." When men
reach that point, greed has gone out of their
service. I make no application of this study
save in the words of the text. Who among
us ?

IV

Will you now turn to the thirteenth verse of
the same chapter: "Ye said also, Behold,
what a weariness is it! and ye have snuffed at
it." There is a process of degradation in the
lives of these men. Profanity, sacrilege, greed,
and then weariness. If a man is seeking for
reward when he opens a door and kindles a
fire, he will soon be tired of the business, and
will say "Oh, what a weariness!" and will
snuff at it; but if, putting forth every effort
and exerting his whole energy, he seeks the
Kingdom for its own sake, he will never com-
plain of fatigue.

I believe this is one of the most remarkable
signs of the present time. Great principles are
revealed in small things and unexpected ways,
and Christendom is saying "The thing is a
weariness," not in actual words, but none the
less certainly. The ritualistic movement is

Christendom saying, "God is a weariness,"
and snuffing at His law. This care concerning
vestments, incense, and the like—what does it
mean? That men are tired of spiritual worship, and must have the sensual side of their
nature pleased and tickled instead thereof.
The stern days of our fathers, when they
worshipped in barns, and sat, cold and cheer-
less, for long hours in spirit conflict with God,
and spirit worship of God—where are they?
Gone, and now we must have everything that
is æsthetic, and when we demand the æsthetic,
we are saying of real worship, "What a weariness it is!" and are asking that things may be
made pleasant and easy for us. Free Church-
men are not exempt from the same snare. All
the unhallowed and ungodly cry for short ser-
mons is evidence that men are saying, "What
a weariness it is!" Scores of people in our
churches to-day, who will hear an opera
through and through—and not once only,—
will pull out their watches and become anxious
and fidgety if a preacher exceeds, by a few
minutes' space, what is recognized as his al-
lotted time.

It is a serious matter—a serious matter.
When men are tired of hearing and meditat-
ing upon the things of God, the fault lies
within; in the background there is greed, and
behind that sacrilege, and behind that again

profanity. Let us search our hearts, and find
whether the things of God have become merely
a duty, a weariness, that we would relinquish
if we dare, and to which we only hold for the
sake of appearances.

V

You will notice in the seventeenth verse of
the second chapter that there is something
further still: "Ye have wearied the Lord
with your words. Yet ye say, Wherein have
we wearied Him? When ye say, Every one
that doeth evil is good in the sight of the
Lord, and He delighteth in them; or, Where
is the God of judgment?" What did they
mean? "Our God is a God of love; there is
no judgment. That man you say is evil, is
good, if you only knew it. God delights in
him." That is beyond weariness and snuffing;
that is treason of the very worst form. That
is a countenancing and an excusing of sin.
That is an attempt to gloss evil and treat it
lightly, as of no importance. When man begins to excuse sin, and to say that it does not
matter so much, that God delights in them
that do evil, that there is no judgment; then
he is committing high treason.

That again is a peculiar sin of our own day.
Find me anywhere a people who are weary of
a strong and robust Christianity and seek æs-

thetic worship, and I find you a people who
cannot bear to be told of the judgment of God.

What are such people really doing ? Lowering the standard of Divine government, and
the moment a man within the Church is guilty
of that, he is flagrantly guilty of high treason
against God.

All this talk about God being such a God of
love that He passes lightly over sin, is the mis-
understanding of what love is. Love is the
sworn foe of sin forever, and the instant God
begins to excuse sin, as we are too often rashly
doing, He proves He does not love man. Nar-
row that down to your own personality, or
rather let me speak of mine. If God excuse
sin in me, and let me go on, just saying, "Well,
he is frail and infirm, it does not matter," God
Himself by such action ensures my ruin. It
is because He is a consuming fire to sin, and
never signs a truce with it within the sphere
of His own kingdom, or in the world anywhere, that He is a God of love ; and directly
people begin to say, " Where is the God of
judgment ? " they are guilty of high treason,
and I believe that has been the peculiar sin of
many years.

The men of our own times whom God has
most signally used have been sons of fire as
well as sons of consolation. Who were the
sons of consolation ? They were Boanerges,

the sons of thunder, and no man is a true son of consolation unless he is also a son of thunder.

A man must have a keen, clear vision of sin, as an enormity of the ages never to be excused, if he is to be tender and compassionate toward the man who is a sinner. That is a false conception of love which imagines God is not a God of judgment.

VI

Again, in the third chapter and the eighth verse, you have the sixth complaint, "Will a man rob God? Yet ye have robbed Me." What a fearful charge! How had they robbed Him? For they said, "Wherein have we robbed Thee?" "In tithes and offerings." In other words, there was a certain Divine claim that God made upon these people; there was a tithe to be given to Him, and they had responded to the demand. "That is what God asked," you say; "surely that was right." Do not make a mistake. People are habitually telling us that God demanded the *tithe*. That is utterly at variance with the true position. God demanded the tithe only as a *minimum*, and they had carelessly given Him what He claimed—the minimum—in tithes and offerings. They had robbed God in that they had not responded to the Divine claim in the spirit in which it was made, but had offered that which was allowed by measurement and rule rather than in the spirit of love.

What is the Divine claim upon Christendom —or Christianity, shall I rather say ? God is not asking you for a tithe. Some give a tithe of their income. That may be the correct thing ; but while there are instances in which it is right, there is a reverse side to the picture. Some men have no business to give a tithe of their earnings—they cannot afford it ; and there are men who are robbing God by giving only a tithe of their incomes. I knew a Congregational Church some years ago in which a man sat in one pew and another man immediately behind him. The income of the first man may roughly be estimated at £10,000 a year, and he and his family gave two pounds conscientiously and regularly every week. He gave an occasional £100 and other sums, but two pounds was his regular weekly gift. The man who sat behind him was a laborer, earning eighteen shillings a week, out of which he gave one shilling. (We have simply got down to money values because they appeal most strongly to the minds of men in this age.) Which man gave the most ? I do not commit any one else to this ; but I told the " man behind " that he had no right, with his wife and family of five bairns, to give a whole shilling out of a weekly wage of eighteen. God does not ask it. Of the man in front—well, his offering was meanness embodied in comparison. A tithe is all right if it is something you feel. If it is something which puts you in danger of being dishonest, it is wrong; and if it is out of harmony with your own success in life, it is absolutely wrong. I do not believe in insisting upon the tithe. God's claim is all —everything to be His. Every coin used selfishly is robbery in the Christian dispensation; and, as I have already said of sacrilege, we should never be compelled to beg from the devil to carry on God's work, if He were not being plundered.

VII

In the thirteenth and fourteenth verses we read, "Your words have been stout against Me, saith the Lord. Yet ye say, Wherein (what) have we spoken so much against Thee? Ye have said, It is vain to serve God; and what profit is it that we have kept His ordinance, and that we have walked mournfully before the Lord of Hosts?" Now, this is the sin of blasphemy. What is blasphemy? The word means to speak injuriously, to say something that shall injure the one against whom you have spoken it; and men have come to use it mostly of Divine things. To blaspheme

is to say that which injures God, and His cause
and His kingdom. He says to these people,
" Your words have been stout against Me,"
that is to say, " You have blasphemed Me
stoutly "; and they say, " Wherein ? " And
He goes on, " You have said, It is vain to serve
God ; and what profit is it that we have kept
His ordinance, and that we have walked ' in
black ' before the Lord ? What is the profit
of all this ? " Do you suppose any of these
people have been saying that in actual words ?
You cannot suppose it for a moment.

The very worst form of blasphemy is the
misrepresentation of God by people who pro-
fess to love His name, and look apparently
with exuberant delight for the coming of His
kingdom. The man who openly blasphemes,
and who, standing under the sun, looks up at
the heavens and says, " I hate God," is far less
dangerous in the influence of his life than the
man who says " I love God " and disobeys
Him. The blasphemy of which to be afraid is
that which joins with the great congregation
in saying, " Thy will be done, Thy kingdom
come," and all the while thwarts the will of
God and denies His kingship within. Oh
brethren, if the Church believed in God's kingdom and God's will, and if the whole catholic
Church of Jesus Christ, on Sunday next, in the
power of the Spirit, breathed that prayer with

unquestionable honesty, how the kingdom would come on apace! It is on account of the blasphemy within our own immediate circle, of men and women who pray the prayer and do not believe in the kingdom, that the thing is hindered, and that the Church of Jesus Christ has become an enervated dilettante in the councils of kings, doing nothing in its corporate capacity to lift the world to heaven and to God.

There are souls, however, to-day, forming God's elect (of whom we shall speak before finishing this series) whom God is using to lay His own foundations, and to do His own work, prior to the coming of the Master to His Church; but Christendom as a whole is at fault and powerless, because Christendom has not believed nor acted upon the teaching of the Master. I know this picture is appalling; but if you can find a brighter one in your outlook, you can do that of which I am absolutely incapable. Do not, however, form final estimates, until we have completed this series of studies. There *is* a bright light, and one which is brighter in the Church than ever it has been in the past decades.

IV

THE DIVINE ATTITUDE

IV

THE DIVINE ATTITUDE

"THE burden of the word of the Lord to Israel by Malachi—I have loved you, saith the Lord" (i. 1, 2). That is the all-comprehensive word which Malachi was sent to proclaim. The love of God! That is the burden. Every word addressed to them concerning the details and conditions of their life springs out of that. In chapter iii. verses 10–12, we have the Divine call: "Bring ye all the tithes into the storehouse, that there may be meat in Mine house, and prove Me now herewith, saith the Lord of Hosts, if I will not open you the windows of heaven, and pour you out a blessing that there shall not be room enough to receive it. And I will rebuke the devourer for your sakes, and he shall not destroy the fruits of your ground; neither shall your vine cast her fruit before the time in the field, saith the Lord of Hosts. And all nations shall call you blessed: for ye shall be a delightsome land, saith the Lord of Hosts." In these two passages, the one declaring the burden of the prophet, and the other giving the direct ap-

peal of Jehovah, we have the call of love to
these people.

We must bear in mind their condition, for
it is a remarkable background to this study.
They were perfectly satisfied men and women,
and yet God, looking at them, charged them
as He did, with sacrilege, profanity, greed,
and so forth. To the people in such a condition, what has God to say ?

I

"I have loved you, saith the Lord." The
word is infinitely stronger than appears upon
the surface. "I have loved you, and do love
you, I have loved you, saith the Lord." This
declaration was made in the time of their sin
and neglect, in the day in which He had
to make the complaint which is so severe and
searching, and yet He says to them : "I have
loved you, saith the Lord." This is the *burden*
of the word of the Lord to Israel by Malachi.
He came to warn them that a day was coming, burning as an oven, wherein all stubble
should be destroyed, because God loved them.
Every message of coming judgment or blessing is a message of love,—whether spoken in
words that sound hard, and harsh, and severe,
revealing to them their true condition, or in
words of tenderness, and comfort and wooing
pathos.

If we consider God's claim to the honor and fear of these people, it is based upon love. Why does God want them to honor Him? Why is He anxious that they should fear Him? Simply to glorify Himself? Nay, verily, but for their blessing and good. "But," says some one, "is it not a Divine prerogative to seek for glory? Is not God, at all times, seeking His own glory?" Most emphatically yes; but what do we mean when we speak of God seeking His own glory? How is God glorified? I sometimes think that we have an idea that our song and presence in heaven will add something to God. Never! You cannot add to God. No tinge of brightness can you put upon the beauty of His character, no greater fullness of love can you give. How then can I glorify Him? God is glorified in the perfect realization on the part of His people of all the gracious purposes of His love for them.

The daisy that lifts its head from the sod to salute the king of day glorifies God, but does it add lustre to the Divine? Assuredly not. It is all that God meant it to be, and God is glorified by the realization of His own purpose. So with us. God wants us to honor and fear Him, because by doing so we shall realize His purpose. Why does He at times lift His rod upon His wayward and wandering children?

Never " willingly," but because it is an absolute necessity for the creation of character.
The severest words of God to man, and His
severest treatment, manifest most perfectly
His unvarying and unchanging love. Let
your mind go back quickly over the history of
God's people, Israel. Mr. Richard Le Gallienne has written a book, " If I were God." I
have often read the history of the ancient people, and felt " if I were God " they would have
been blotted out. How conclusively that
proves that neither Mr. Le Gallienne nor I
know of what we talk when we propose such
an hypothesis. And yet we can only argue of
themes of the infinite wisdom and love by such
daring leaps in the dark. Let us always con-
fess when we cannot understand His methods
that it is because we are finite, and He is infinite.

" Forty years was I grieved with this gener-
ation." Read the history of the forty years
and see how He treated them ! He fed them,
He carried them through all the days, He bore
with their murmurings and patiently waited
for them. He took all their rebellion and suf-
fered it in long-suffering patience. He pro-
tected them during the watches of the night,
and waited for them at the doors of the morning, and carried them through all the years—
years in which He was grieved with them. Let

us never forget this burden of love. Is it not
this attitude of God that makes their attitude
to Him so awful, and, moreover, is not the
key-word of Malachi the one that gives its
character to the whole book, so that the
prophecy of Malachi to us is not a dirge as it
would be, if we only read of their condition;
but a shout of triumph because God says, "I
have loved you"? That is the key-word to
the whole prophecy, and with the background
of our previous consideration, how brightly
and beautifully the Divine love and tenderness shine out as we hear that word of the
prophet.

This is an eternal truth—each word and
deed and movement of God toward man is of
infinite love. It is not always that men have
understood this as clearly as did Malachi.
Preachers sometimes forget it; but the truth
stands that every God-called, ordained, inspired messenger of Divine things may approach the people to whom he speaks, saying,
"The burden of the word of the Lord to *you :*
I have loved you, saith the Lord."

II

Let us now turn from the key-word to the
special call. He has made His complaint; He
has heard their perpetual responses, coming in

that awful monotone—" Wherein ? " and now
He says to them by the mouth of His servant:
" Bring ye all the tithes into the storehouse
that there may be meat in Mine house, and
prove Me now herewith, saith the Lord of
Hosts, if I will not open you the windows of
heaven, and pour you out a blessing that there
shall not be room enough to receive it. And
I will rebuke the devourer for your sakes, and
he shall not destroy the fruits of your ground,
neither shall your vine cast her fruit before
the time in the field, saith the Lord of Hosts.
And all nations shall call you blessed ; for ye
shall be a delightsome land, saith the Lord of
Hosts." We have in these three verses four
notes :—

(1) The call of God : " Bring ye all the
tithes into the storehouse."

(2) The challenge of God : " And prove Me
now herewith, saith the Lord of
Hosts."

(3) The promise of God : " I will open you
the windows of heaven, and pour you
out a blessing that there shall not be
room enough to receive it ; and I will
rebuke the devourer for your sakes,
and he shall not destroy the fruits of
your ground, neither shall your vine
cast her fruit before the time in the
field."

(4) The result: "And all nations shall call
you blessed; for ye shall be a delightsome land, saith the Lord of Hosts."
Remembering the condition of this people,
rebellious, and yet perfectly satisfied with their
own position, let us ponder this message of
God to them.

i. First, there is the call: "Bring all the
tithes into the storehouse." There were
necessarily two sides to the covenant existing
between God and the nation. There were
mutual obligations. His promises were made
upon conditions. If they failed to fulfill these
conditions, the covenant was broken. They
had failed, and yet He in grace called them to
a renewal by the way of return to obedience.
"Bring all the tithes into the storehouse."
What is God really asking for? Does He
want a tenth part of their wheat, of their
flocks, of their possessions, simply for Himself,
to possess it? Assuredly not. He asks for
the tenth part as a proof that they recognize
His love toward them. The tithe is only
valuable as a recognition of love, and the only
force which is strong enough to provide the
tithe is the consciousness of the truth of that
first word of Malachi: "I have loved you,
saith the Lord." If these people forget God
loves, they will very soon forget to bring the
tithe; and the only service that God seeks

is the service of love that responds to His
love.

He asks for the "whole tithe." It is an infinitely better word than "all the tithes."
That is a mathematical phrase, and seems to
suggest a mathematical or mechanical religion,
but the "whole tithe" means not only the
produce of their land and labor, not only the
outward form, but its inner intention. "All
the tithes" is not necessarily "the whole
tithe."

Supposing one of these men had possessed a
hundred shekels. Has he not fulfilled the
Divine requirement when he has brought of
these hundred, *ten* for God, for mathematically
that is the tithe? No! out of the hundred,
ten perfect shekels may be placed upon the
altar, the coins genuine to the eye of man, but
in God's sight—counterfeit. They did not
constitute "the whole." What was lacking?
The recognition of love. There was not the
response of love to love for which God is always asking: "Bring the whole tithe." There
is an apparent wholeness to us that is the
utterest fraud in the sight of God. There is a
mechanical correctness, devoid of essential
love, which God spurns. "Bring the whole
tithe," and bring it in the right way ; let it
come as the recognition of His love. When it
is thus brought, it means, borrowing a sen-

tence from the New Testament, "We love Him, because He first loved us." Our love is but the offspring of His love, our tithe given, a recognition of His all bestowed.

God is calling for the investiture of form with power, and the one power which God recognizes is that of love. If we would see our organizations invested with power they must be invested with love, and the preacher is to preach, and the worker to work, not to give God a mechanical quantity, but in response to love. When that is an established fact the tithes are brought into the storehouse.

ii. Now for the challenge : " Prove Me now herewith." Get to know Me by answering My love with your love; respond to the love that is ever upon you, even in your rebellion and sin, with love, and by that response be admitted into love and knowledge and understanding. " Prove Me now herewith." This was God's challenge to the people.

iii. Mark the promise: " Prove Me if I will not open you the windows of heaven, and pour you out a blessing that there shall not be room enough to receive it. " The source of blessing —heaven's windows open; the measure of blessing—until there shall not be room enough to receive it. Now the word really is, until there shall not be a " sufficiency."

It is possible that our translators both in the

Authorized and Revised versions have caught
the true spirit of the word, but it is somewhat
ambiguous. One daring commentator of other
days suggests that it should read: "Prove
Me now herewith, saith God, till there shall
not be a sufficiency," "that is to say," says the
writer, "God will keep on pouring blessing
out until His own sufficiency ends; and when
can that be? Never!" The writer says this
is the most remarkable figure in the whole
book. It is a magnificent conception even if
it does not catch the first and true meaning of
the word. The thought is that of the "prodi-
gality" of Divine love. It runs over every
measure, and goes before us, and encompasses
us even in our sin, and He says: "If you will
but bring the tithe, acknowledge the love, and
look up and say 'Eternal Love, we love,' I will
open the windows of heaven and pour out a
blessing that you cannot receive it."

What else? "I will rebuke the devourer."
The insect that is destroying your crops I will
destroy for your sakes. That word "rebuke"
is the same which is used in the second chapter and the third verse, translated there: "Behold, I will *corrupt* your seed." Corrupt is
the correct word. Lift that word and put it
in here. "I will *corrupt* the devourer." The
punishment was that all the seed was to be
corrupt. The blessing was that not the seed,

but the devourer was to be corrupted. "I will corrupt the devourer."

And then follows that perfect figure of beauty and strength: "Neither shall your vine cast her fruit before the time in the field."

iv. What is to be the result of this blessing? "All nations shall call you happy." God says that when His people return to Him, bringing the tithes, and He returns to them in blessing, there is to be a great consensus of opinion as to their condition. All the nations of the world will make an admission concerning them. There shall be none who shall deny their blessedness and happiness. "All nations shall call you blessed." The world is waiting for that. I do not think it has ever seen it. The blessing of God for the people has not been seen in Israel's history or in the history of the Christian Church. We have never reached it. I think it will come when the King comes, and in His own Kingdom He sets up the blessings of love which He described in the Sermon on the Mount; then all the nations shall say, "Happy is the people whose God is the Lord."

And what more? "Yours shall be a delightsome land," perfect in itself, the ideal realized as the result of obedience.

III

What are the thoughts which this study of
the Divine attitude suggests for us? First,
that of the great eternal love. Notwithstand-
ing all the varied and varying conditions of
humanity, love underlies all the Divine deal-
ings, and love still marks the attitude of God
to His people despite their failures, their rebellion, alas! alas! so often evident. There is a
very considerable tendency to-day, on the part
of the people whose eyes are open, and who
are in a measure responding to the Divine call,
to become a clique, or class, and look down on
the failure of their brethren and sisters who
are living the lower life of formalism. Directly you find yourself looking down with
lack of love upon your fellow Christians, rest
assured that you are departing from that very
blessing of which you have been proud.

God is saying to us: "I have loved you."
That is why He never gives you any rest about
that particular habit, which appears so inno-
cent, and yet which is the very crux of the
controversy between you and Himself. "I
have loved you, saith the Lord." It is the infinite proof of love when God does not let you
rest. It is as dangerous to let your conscience
assume a state of apathy as it would be to al-
low a sleepy man to slumber in the snows of

the Sierras. Have you a controversy with
God which has been going on for weeks, aye,
for months, and even years, until you are
weary of it, and in danger of growing rebellious because of His interference—Hold, man!
—"I have loved you!" If God had not loved
you, He would have left you to your own de-
vices and evil. Your evil habit, selfish indul-
gence, is your enemy, and while God brings
you back to this point, time after time, He is
proving His love for your soul. "I have loved
you." We must live in the element of this
Divine love.

The next lesson I gather is that of the relation which exists between tithe and blessing.
"Bring the tithe, and I will open the windows
of heaven." How perpetually people in prayer-
meetings pray the promise and forget the conditions. We pray: "Open the windows of
heaven and pour us out a blessing," and God
replies: "Bring the tithes." It is as though
God said to you: "It is for you to open the
windows." What? the windows of heaven?
Yes! heaven's windows always swing upon
love's hinges. There is a very radical and
practical application of this phrase, which one
is slow to make and yet it must be made. Do
not imagine because we are living in a spiritual dispensation we are no longer bound in
the matter of material giving. We are to

bring the tithes. It is not the tithe that God asks from you, but everything! You may make a proportionate statement of it if you will. As the Christian dispensation is greater than the Jewish, so must my giving be greater than a tithe, and when you have worked out the first ratio you will begin to understand the second. When men come and say, " Here we are, our interests, ourselves, our business— everything," then the windows of heaven are never shut—never!

I want you to see the subtle connection between tithe and blessing. You know that little verse that people sing in Conventions —

> " My all is on the altar,
> I'm waiting for the fire."

It is an absolute absurdity. Nobody ever waited for the fire when all was on the altar. Let a man sing if he like —

> " A part is on the altar.
> I'm waiting for the fire."

I do not know that he ought to waste the time in singing even that, but bestir himself to get the other portion on the altar. That is his business. When you and I put our *all* upon the altar the fire falls directly. You read in the story of Elijah how the fire descended straightway. God's conditions being fulfilled —God's promises never halt. It is you and I

that are maimed, and lame, and halt. God
does not halt. "Bring the tithes," and the
moment they come the windows open and the
showers of blessing descend. That is a law
which applies equally to the individual, to the
nation, to the Church, and to the world. We
begin with ourselves. When my all is upon
the altar, then the windows of heaven are
open and the blessing descends. When the
Church brings the tithe into the storehouse,
and acknowledging and honoring Him, sweeps
away all methods that so detract from the fulfillment of her mission and says, "Only for
Thy glory do I exist," then the blessing is
given. *Man's tithes and God's windows.*

Then we must go further still and notice,
not only the relationship between tithe and
blessing, but that between love and tithe.
Tithes never reach the storehouse except in
response to love. Mechanical religion cannot
last; it always becomes weary and ceases. I
may preach to you and use every argument I
know as to your giving to God. You will
never do it in response to human eloquence.
When do men give to God? When they have
a true vision of Him. That is the secret of
giving tithes, and that, in its turn, is the secret
of the opening of heaven's windows.

Out of that grows another question. How
can we love? Only as we prove God in the

path of obedience. This is a burden laid upon my own heart perpetually. I love God in proportion as I obey Him. The first steps may be taken in the dark without seeing a reason, but take them, and you begin to see the wisdom and tenderness, and compassion, and love of God. I love when I obey, and when I love, I obey. Which is cause and which is effect? There is an inter-relation in the progress of Christian love. But obedience is the first thing. In the beginning, seek first the Kingdom, and when the soul seeks the Kingdom by obeying the King, the soul discovers the Father, and discovering the Father obeys more readily, and obeying more readily, has a larger revelation which makes obedience easy and the horizon greater. We are changed from glory into glory, and at last we shall be like Him, and obey perfectly. Such is the Divine arrangement.

A delightsome land in the mind of God is acknowledged happy by the nations. How is it that the world is so sick and tired of Christianity? How is it that men outside the Church have come to look upon us with disdain? Is it not so? You business men, tell me, is there not a sort of pity in the heart of scores of worldly men for Christian men today? Why is this? It is the fault of the Church, of the people themselves, not the creed. " Give me," said John Wesley, " a hundred men who love God with all their hearts, and fear nothing but sin, and I will move the world." People who saw and mocked them in the early days grew to love them, and came to say: " These people have what we have not; we will go with them, for God is with them." Again and again God has raised up a despised and unknown people to render concrete the blessings of His Kingdom and Government; and where this has been done the world has said, " This is a delightsome land," and where the world has ceased to say that, it is because the people have wandered away from Him. Brethren, if the Church of Jesus Christ in this land returned to the Kingdom to-morrow morning, and every one of its members returned to the Kingship of Jesus Christ, the whole country would be impressed straightway, and within one twelvemonth would say, " These are the people, this is the delightsome land, these the men and women of delights." Some one says to me: " What do you mean by returning to the Kingdom? Everything divided, having all things in common?" I mean one thing when I say returning to the Kingdom. Let them return to love, to the love " that suffereth long and is kind—that thinketh no evil, rejoiceth not in iniquity, but rejoiceth in the truth; beareth all things, believeth all

things, hopeth all things." Love like that, and
you will never say a bitter thing about an ab-
sent neighbor! You will never suffer an un-
kind thing to be said about some one "afar
off." That is the place to begin, and if the
Church of Jesus Christ did but reveal His will
in all its breadth, and beauty of love, the nations would begin to say, "This is a delightsome land; surely God is with this people, we
will go with them also."

This is God's call to the Church, with its
sleeping, slumbering energies. Oh yes, one
must put it like that, because if the Church,
the great company of men and women in the
world to-day, who name the name of Christ,
were living in the Kingdom, actuated by the
love of God, responding to the forces of His
Spirit, we could settle every question straightway. God is brooding over His sleeping people, His sleeping Church, and saying, "I have
loved you." "Bring ye all the tithes into the
storehouse, that there may be meat in Mine
house, and prove Me now herewith, saith the
Lord of Hosts, if I will not open you the windows of heaven, and pour you out a blessing,
that there shall not be room enough to receive
it. And I will rebuke the devourer for your
sakes, and he shall not destroy the fruits of
your ground; neither shall your vine cast her
fruit before the time in the field, saith the

Lord of Hosts.   And all nations shall call you
blessed : for ye shall be a delightsome land,
saith the Lord of Hosts."   " Prove Me," says
God.   There is one question for us: " Who
hears the Divine call ? and hearing, who will
respond ? "

V

THE ELECT REMNANT

V

THE ELECT REMNANT

GOD has never left Himself without a definite and clear witness to the truths upon which the well-being of humanity is based. In the first chapter of John's gospel, verses four and five, we read: "In Him was life, and the life was the light of men. And the light shineth in darkness, and the darkness comprehended it not." The Revised Version has altered the word "comprehended" to "apprehended"; and I am not perfectly sure that it has made the passage more luminous by the alteration. The idea of the verse is not that the darkness was not able to understand the light; but that the darkness never succeeded in overtaking and extinguishing the light. "The light shineth in darkness, and the darkness comprehended it not," that is—did not apprehend, overtake, or put out. There have been times in the history of man when it has seemed as though the whole world has been given over to darkness; but it has never really been so. The light of God has ever been shining. Elijah once said in the agony of his disap-

pointed spirit, "I, even I, only am left," and
God said to him, "I have left Me seven thousand in Israel, all the knees which have not
bowed unto Baal." Thus in every successive
age, when it has seemed for a while as though
God were beaten out of His own world, and
black and impenetrable darkness had com-
pletely overpowered the light, that has only
been the false vision of men and women who
have not been able to enclose the Divine horizon at one glance. Somewhere or other, although it may not have been discernible to
the ordinary vision, the light has still been
burning.

It was so in the days of Malachi. Notwith-
standing all the fearful darkness that had
settled upon the nation, God had His own
people, His Elect Remnant; and through them
the light still shone, and witness was still
borne to the great truths and principles upon
which all the Divine activity is based for the
well-being of man. It is on the shining of the
Divine light in that dark period of the history
of the ancient people of God that we shall now
fix our attention. We shall consider firstly
the Elect Remnant as it is revealed in these
verses; then we shall notice the Divine attitude toward that Remnant; and lastly, hear
the Divine word spoken concerning them.

I

" *Then* they that feared the Lord spake often one to another." Right in the midst of that day—when the nation, considered as a whole, had passed into the region of life characterized by perfect self-satisfaction, and by the fact that they brought no satisfaction to the Divine Heart—God pronounced His complaint against them, and they, almost speechless with incredulity, looked into His face and said, "*Wherein?*" Then there existed a feeble yet faithful few who were the light-bearers of God.

Let us notice the character of this Elect Remnant: "They that feared." At the close of the sixteenth verse of the third chapter, that first fact is not only repeated, but emphasized by the addition of another: "They that feared the Lord, *and that thought upon His name.*" We have here a revelation of the character of these people, which is full of interest and of meaning. "They feared the Lord, and thought upon His name."

Let us take the first part of that description. If you turn back to the sixth verse of the first chapter, you will find that in the opening note of the Divine complaint the prophet said: "A son honoreth his father, and a servant his master; if, then, I be a Father, where is Mine

honor? and if I be a Master, where is My
fear?" Here is a company that *have* "feared
the Lord," and *have* "thought upon His
name"; so that amid all the mass of people
who had lost the sense of their fear to their
Master, there was an Elect Remnant, a select
few, who not only called Him "Master," but
also feared Him. The thought of fear is
linked, then, with the word master, and with
all that that word implies. If you speak of a
master, you at once think of a servant; and
while the relationship of the master to the
servant is that of authority and will and guid-
ance, the relation of the servant to the master
is that of obedience and service. Bearing this
in mind, you notice that service is looked upon
here rather as condition than action. Character is marked in this word, "They that feared
the Lord"; they that lived within the conscious realm of the Divine, and responded to
that claim; that number of units in the great
crowd who recognized the Divine Kingship, not
merely as theory, or as something of which
they made a boast to other people, but as the
power in which they lived their lives and
spent all their days: "They feared the Lord."
There were men and women all around making offerings, and crowding the courts of the
temple at the hour of worship. Among those
who came, God detected the men and women

who really feared, and He selected only the
gifts of those who presented something—not
as an attempt to make up what they lacked in
character, but as an output of character, and
as a revelation of what they were within
themselves. "They feared the Lord."

Let us now turn to the second part of this
description: "They thought upon His name."
The word "thought" is one of intense meaning, and I should like to trace it in one or two
passages of Scripture in order that we may
more clearly understand it.

In the seventeenth verse of the thirteenth
chapter of Isaiah we read: "Behold, I will stir
up the Medes against them, which shall not
regard silver; and as for gold, they shall not
delight in it." The only purpose for which we
have turned to this verse is that we may extract
the word "regard" from it, and see how it is
used in this particular case. The Medes will
not "regard" silver—that is to say, that they
will set no value on silver. The Medes, stirred
up against the ancient people of God, will not
be bought off by silver. They do not set any
value upon it, they do not "regard" it. The
connection between this thought and that of
our text is centered in the fact that the Hebrew
word translated "think" in Malachi is exactly
the same word which is translated "regard"
in Isaiah. They thought upon His name, they

regarded His name, they set a value upon His name.

Take another case in which the same word is again translated "regard." Isaiah xxxiii. 8, "The highways lie waste, the wayfaring man ceaseth: he hath broken the Covenant, he hath despised the cities, he *regardeth* no man." That is, he sets no value upon man. The word is identical with that translated in Malachi: "They that thought upon the Lord" —that is to say, what these people did not do concerning man, the Elect Remnant did concerning God. I do not say there is any connection between these passages; we are simply getting the light of them upon a particular word in our present study. They regarded God, they set a value upon Him. In the terrible day described by Isaiah the personal man was not regarded, he was accounted as "nothing worth," valueless; but this Elect Remnant set regard upon the name of the Lord; they did for that Name what the Medes did not do for silver, and what was not done for man in the days of which Isaiah writes.

In the same prophecy a very remarkable case occurs. Isaiah liii. 3: "He is despised and rejected of men; a Man of sorrows, and acquainted with grief: and we hid as it were our faces from Him; He was despised, and we esteemed Him not." "Esteemed" is the word; it is the same Hebrew word translated "thought" in Malachi. You see the word again almost more wonderfully presented here than in other instances. " We *esteemed* Him not." We thought nothing of Him; we set no value upon Him; His worth in our sight was nothing, and we spurned Him from us. He came to His own, and they received Him not; they perceived no beauty in Him that they should desire Him. But the Elect Remnant esteemed the name of the Lord; they " thought upon His name "—they set a high value thereon.

To follow this thought a little further in order that we may get additional light upon it, turn to the letter of Paul to the Philippians, iv. 8: " Finally, brethren, whatsoever things are true, whatsoever things are honest, whatsoever things are just, whatsoever things are pure, whatsoever things are lovely, whatsoever things are of good report; if there be any virtue, and if there be any praise, think on these things." The Greek word translated " think " here is a word which means " Take an inventory." What are the things of which men, as a rule, take an inventory? Things which they value; and Paul, in writing, is practically saying, " Do not reckon as riches things perishing; but those things which make you rich indeed, the things which are true, honest, just, pure, lovely, of good report, take an inventory of these, keep your mind upon them, set a value upon them." In the Septuagint the translators have taken this word which Paul uses, and have used it in the three cases in Isaiah—to which we have already referred—so that when you read, "These men *thought* on the name of the Lord," it is not a matter of little moment; they did not simply meditate upon His name, and meet together to endeavor to comprehend its deep riches. All this I believe they did; but their position as described by this word is far more wonderful than that. It is that they set value upon the name of the Lord, esteemed it, made an inventory in it, accounted it as their property, wealth, riches. It was the chief thing; nothing else was worth consideration to these faithful people. They took an inventory in the name of the Lord.

That leads us to another point. The Master Himself, in the Sermon on the Mount, chronicled in Matthew v., vi., vii., gave utterance to these words : "Where your treasure is, there will your heart be also." That is one of the sayings of Jesus Christ which is of such simplicity that I may use it as an everyday truth in my experience, and yet it is at the same time the statement of a great fundamental principle in all human life. "Where your treasure is, there will your heart be also." The

masses of the people of Malachi's day found
their treasure in their possessions, in their nationality, and in the temple, and consequently
their hearts reached no higher altitude than
the platform of things mundane; but the Elect
Remnant set store by the name of the great
Jehovah, and their hearts were therefore
homed in God.

Turn once more to Proverbs xxiii. 7, where
these words occur: "As a man thinketh in his
heart, so is he." These people thought upon
the name of the Lord, and where their treasure was their heart nestled, the result being
that their whole life assumed form and character from their conception of treasure, and
from the things upon which their hearts medi-
tated.

"They thought upon the name of the Lord."
That word reveals a company of people who
valued the Name, and counted it as their chief
treasure, with the result that their character
became responsive to all that the Name signi-
fied, and their life grew in closer correspondence to the will of God.

What a name was that on which they thus
thought may be gathered from a study of the
titles associated therewith in the mind of the
Hebrew. *Jehovah-Jireh*—The Lord will provide; *Jehovah-Tsidkenu*—The Lord our righteousness; *Jehovah-Shalom*—The Lord send

peace; *Jehovah-Nissi*—The Lord our banner; *Jehovah-Shammah*—The Lord is there. Search the matter out for yourselves, and you will find that these people had a marvellous heritage in the name of Jehovah. He had revealed Himself by names continually, and there had been along the line of their history new beauty, new glory, perpetually breaking out by means of these very names by which God had approached them time after time. These people thought upon the name of the Lord, of His provision for them; His righteousness; His banner, the proof of love in His conflict with sin; of His presence, and, thinking of these things, their nature was transformed into correspondence with His own, so that they became righteous, and they became peaceful, and they became quiet in the presence of their faithful God. So much for the character of this Elect Remnant.

A word or two concerning their occupation. "They that feared the Lord spake one to another." The word "often" is omitted in the Revised Version, and does not occur in the original. It is one of those words that seem to add to, but in reality detract from, the meaning of the text. "Spake often one to another" admits of gaps in the fellowship. "Spake one to another" tells the whole story of their communication, for it marks the attitude rather than the occupation of a life. "They spake one to another." It is the great statement of fellowship, of the gathering together in a community of hearts holding the same treasure, of characters that were growing into the same likeness; it is the statement of a great necessity, darkness all around, light becomes focused; evil spreading its ramifications on every hand, children of righteousness come close together. "They spake one to another;" and of what did they speak? Surely concerning that of which they thought; they spoke of His name, their mutual possession in that name, their mutual joy in that name, their mutual sorrow by reason of the fact that that name was being blasphemed by the nation they were bound to love, because they themselves formed a part of it.

Mark, the great value of this fellowship of kindred spirits lay in the fact that they were strong by reason thereof. Scattered souls are ever weaker than those bound together in feeling, and principle, and desire. This Elect Remnant, so weak and feeble that I venture to say that none but God would have found it, or known it existed, was the one thing that saved the nation from absolute and total wreckage and deplorable ruin—the little group of souls who feared the Lord, and who gathered together to speak to each other concern-

ing Him. Just notice in passing that it was
not a prayer-meeting; it was a fellowship-
meeting, if a meeting at all. I do not say
these people did not pray; but I am much in-
clined to think that they had passed into the
higher realm of prayer, to which men and
women always pass under the stress of adver-
sity, when the storm-clouds threaten to envelop
their lives. Their gatherings were the means
for fellowship rather than the place for peti-
tion, and " they spake one to another."

II

Secondly, what is the Divine attitude toward this Elect Remnant? "The Lord
hearkened and *heard*." Please to omit the
word "it"! The words "hearkened" and
" heard " are not identical; there is a great
necessity that they should both appear. He
hearkened—He heard. The root meaning of
" hearkened " is to prick the ears. You have
known what it is to drive a horse which is
familiar with your voice and loves you. After
travelling several miles along your journey
you suddenly speak, and you see the animal's
ears instantly pricking. That is the true
meaning of the word "hearkened"—pricking the ears. "The Lord hearkened." Of
course, these illustrations appear to be degrad-
ing to the thought of the Divine, and yet, the

whole of human speech is human; we have
not yet learned the language of the spirit
world, we have not yet begun to spell out
the alphabet of the true communication between God and those who inhabit that world;
we are bound to take these words in all their
human sense. God condescends to take up
the words with which we are most familiar
and teach us through this avenue, because we
could not understand if He did not condense
the great thoughts of His mind into the com-
pass of simple language.

"The Lord hearkened." Mark the extreme
sensitiveness of the Divine love. *Here* is a
crowd of people bringing their offerings, ut-
tering their prayers, thronging the courts of
the temple; and the prophet is telling them
of their sin, and charging them with sacrilege,
profanity, and so forth, and they, with their
faces transformed into veritable notes of in-
terrogation, and stamped with surprise, reply:
"Wherein?" *Over there* is a group who have
met together to talk about God. To them He
hearkened. This teaches the sensitiveness of
the eternal love.

The word translated "heard" means He
bent over them in order that He might miss
no syllable of their conversation. The first is
a word that marks arrest—"He hearkened!"
The second shows the infinite patience of God;

listening to their words as they talked, not to
Him, but to one another about Him—" The
Lord heard." While the word " hearkened "
marks the sensitiveness of the Divine love, the
word " heard" marks the strength of that
love. These are companion thoughts, they always go together. That is not strong love
which is vehement, passionate, loud, and bois-
terous. Strong love is the love of the soft
footfall, and the beautiful patience that
watches with unceasing wakefulness by the
bedside of the sick, and nurses the suffering and
almost flickering life back to health and
strength. That is strong love—the love which
through long and weary nights of watchful-
ness wins the life from the black angel Death.
" The Lord heard "—He bent over them and
attended to them, caught every syllable that
fell from their lips, every intonation and inflection of their voices; and amid all the dis-
cord of that awful day in which man had
wandered from Him, and forgotten Him, here
was music for Him, something satisfying even
to His heart—an Elect Remnant that feared
Him, thought upon His name, and spake one
to another.

The Lord hearkened and heard, and a Book
of Remembrance was written before Him ; for
" them that feared the Lord, and thought upon
His name," a Book of Remembrance, God's

Scroll of Honor. The highest privilege that could be conferred upon the men of that or any age is that their names should be written therein. When the disciples came back from their mission, and said, "Master, even the devils are subject to us," Christ replied, "Rejoice rather that your names are written in heaven." We had not yet learned to see these things as we shall do some day, when all the wrongs of earth are righted, and we reach consummation and finality. There is only one Scroll of Honor, and it is never kept on the earth, but in the heavens; and in that Book of Remembrance have been written the names of those who, amidst rampant apostasy, have been faithful; amidst the prevalence of darkness have witnessed to the light; amidst the seeming conquest of evil have been true to righteousness and God. Those names are inscribed in God's Book of Remembrance in indelible ink, and that little group of souls, the Elect Remnant, who feared Him and thought upon His name, although they little knew it, their names were being written in the Book of Remembrance.

III

Take the last point and notice the Divine determination concerning these people. "They shall be Mine, saith the Lord in that day I

act." There has been some difficulty about
this translation. The Revised has altered the
old form with some apparent hesitation. The
Hebrew word translated "make" or "do
make" is one that is used in the broadest possible sense to indicate activity, and the reference here is undoubtedly to the day when God
will act. Some people are afraid lest the
thought of God's people being His jewels
should be lost by this rendering, but it is not.
If you read it as it is in the Authorized, "They
shall be Mine, saith the Lord, in that day
when I make up My jewels," you have an idea
conveyed to your mind that a day is coming
when God will gather His jewels and make
them up into one great whole, but this, while
perfectly true, is nevertheless a very partial
idea. The real idea is best expressed thus:
"They shall be Mine, saith the Lord in the
day when I act—My jewels." The word
"jewels" is in the nominative case in apposi-
tion to the pronoun "they," at the beginning
of the sentence, "They shall be Mine in the
day when I act, My special treasure." So that
you have not merely the assuring and blessed
word that God will gather these people together, His own precious treasure; but there
is another word, which goes deeper and is
more full of blessed assurance still, that God
is coming "to do"—"to act," coming in upon

all this indifference to set it right; and God
says, "In the day I act, these people who have
been faithful, and have feared My name, and
thought upon My name, shall be My special
treasure." You see there is nothing lost. We
still have the sweet assurance that He will
gather His own people as His jewels; but we
have also the great assertion that He is coming to act, that while the present is man's day,
God's day lies ahead. He will manifest Himself in greater power and glory than ever before. In that day they shall be Mine, My
jewels, My special treasure."

Beside the places in which Israel is spoken
of as such, this word "special treasure," only
occurs twice in the Bible. First it is used of
"David's treasures laid up for building the
temple" (1 Chron. xxix. 3), and in the other
place it is used in Ecclesiastes ii. 8 : "And the
peculiar treasure of kings and of the provinces."
David stored away the precious things for the
building of the temple; God is storing away
His special treasure for the construction of His
own Kingdom. Kings had treasures upon
which they set special value; God has His
also, upon which *He* sets special value, human
character responsive to the Divine will, fearing
Him and thinking upon His name; and of the
men and women of such character He declares,
"They shall be Mine." Thus you have the

announcement that God has not forsaken His
world, and the further declaration that when
He comes to consummate His purposes, the
faithful ones amid faithless days, shall be His
—His special treasure.

From that study of the Elect Remnant let
us gather one or two thoughts for ourselves.
God has His Elect Remnant to-day in those
who fear Him and think upon His name.   I
am not going to attempt, by any word I say,
to measure that Remnant, and I rejoice that it
has never been revealed to man in any dispensation.   It has always been known only and
exclusively to the Divine heart, to the Divine
love.   If you show me a few people who say,
" We are the Elect Remnant, we are the Remnant, we are the people who pronounce words
in this particular way, or look in that particular direction, we are the people of God's Elect
Remnant "—the claim is the sufficient proof of
its falseness ! Never ! God's Elect Remnant
in this age is not marked off by any little human boundary of sect or party.   God has His
faithful souls in the Roman Catholic Church.
Let us not blunder about that.   I, for one, will
not join in all the hateful, indiscriminate out-
cry against Roman Catholics.   The Romish
system is one of the most awful the world has
ever seen ; but in that system are men who
were born in it, and are devout in it, and are

better than it, who form part of God's Elect
Remnant. I have known such. You will find
part of them in the great Anglican Church of
this country; thank God there are thousands
in that Church who must be, by virtue of the
saintliness and tenderness and compassion of
their lives, God's Elect Remnant. You find
them in all sections of the Free Church, and a
great number, alas! outside the Church alto-
gether. No one Church can mark off the Remnant of God. Men entitled to that distinction
are found everywhere. What are their char-
acteristics? Men who fear Him and who are
so conscious of His Kingdom that they live in
it; and of His Mastership that they respond
to it. Not the men and women who say
"Lord, Lord," but they who do the things that
God approves. Not the great heterogeneous
crowd that bow the head, and say "Thy Kingdom come, Thy will be done"; but the saintly
souls in whose life the Kingdom *is* come, and
the will *is* being done.

These are His Elect people, and thank God,
they are not confined to one section of this
poor, broken-up, fragmentary Christendom of
ours, but are everywhere. Yet, is it not important that such should gather together to-
day in closest fellowship? That we should
fear His name, and think upon His name,
and learn to set greater value upon His name

than upon any other? Is it not high time that
we ceased to attempt, either by picnic in
Switzerland, or conference at home, to arrange
an organic union? Is it not better that we
should recognize and nourish the true unity of
heart that exists between those who think
upon His name, and take an inventory, not in
the wealth, nor in the organizations of to-day,
but in that great Eternal Name which is a
strong tower of righteousness?

If in this connection I make any plea, it is
this : That in this day of large failure, those
who love the Lord Jesus Christ in sincerity
and truth—and that term is synonymous with
the Old Testament one, " They that feared the
Lord "—should come together, and enjoy this
fellowship, this oneness of heart. Take the
old declaration and put it in the new dispensation : " The Lord hearkened and the Lord
heard ; " that marks God's present interest, and
His great promise made concerning such is
still " They shall be Mine in that day when I
act." What interests God most in this age?
I am bold to assert that there is nothing more
interesting to the heart of the Divine than the
" closing together " of Christian souls, not to
try to make their creeds fit in, or their organizations coalesce ; but in order that there may
be a creation of character that is to be the
shining of the Divine light amid the darkness

of the world. The Lord hears, and no syllable whispered one to the other, that has in it the element of permanence, does His ear ever miss, because He is righteousness and love; and of the people who utter these words, He says, "They shall be Mine in the day when I act, My special treasure."

Surely it is such souls that salt and season all the earth. The little company gathered together when Jesus came, who were they? The Elect Remnant; Zacharias and Elizabeth; Joseph and Mary; Simeon and Anna; Shepherds on the plains, and Wise Men from afar —larger than a Jewish nationality, wider afield than the strip of land called Palestine— God's Elect souls united by no bond of human organization, held together by no creed of human manufacture, but *one* in that "they feared the Lord, and thought upon His name."

And so, when dawns God's next great day —and some of us believe the dawning very near—the Elect Remnant will be found, not bound together by human organizations, not held by creeds; but from the North and the South, from the East and from the West, from all lands and climes, from all the churches, shall come *the* Church—God's Remnant, fearing Him and thinking upon His name.

VI

THE FINAL WORD

VI

THE FINAL WORD

" FOR, behold, the day cometh, that shall
burn as an oven; and all the proud, yea, and
all that do wickedly, shall be stubble: and the
day that cometh shall burn them up, saith the
Lord of Hosts, that it shall leave them neither
root nor branch. But unto you that fear My
name shall the Sun of righteousness arise with
healing in His wings; and ye shall go forth,
and grow up as calves of the stall. And ye
shall tread down the wicked; for they shall
be ashes under the soles of your feet in the
day that I shall do this, saith the Lord of
Hosts. Remember ye the law of Moses my
servant, which I commanded unto him in
Horeb for all Israel, with the statutes and
judgments. Behold, I will send you Elijah
the prophet before the coming of the great
and dreadful day of the Lord; and he shall
turn the heart of the fathers to the children,
and the heart of the children to their fathers,
lest I come and smite the earth with a curse "
(Malachi iv.).

" With a curse "—so ends this prophecy of
Malachi. After this there is to be no prophetic

voice, no direct message from God for over
four hundred years. It is of the utmost importance that the word shall be one that shall
arrest attention, one possessed of the power to
abide. What is it ? The word " *curse.*" This
is, moreover, the last word of the Old Testament, and that, I believe, of Divine purpose,
with solemn intention. As we look at it a
little more closely, we shall see, that behind
the fact that the canon ends thus, lies the
tenderness of the Divine heart. God's last
message to these people is intended to arouse
them, in order that the threatened curse may
never rest upon them. Let us proceed to consider :—

(1) The final word itself.

(2) The Gospel of love by which it is per-
meated.

(3) The great announcement : " Behold, the
day cometh."

I

The Final Word.—The whole history of
man to this point is one of failure ; the only
word therefore that is possible from the God
of all perfection, as revealing His attitude toward this state of things, is the word " curse."
Read that history from the standpoint of the
Divine, and observe how constantly it mani-
fests the faithfulness of God, the tenderness of

His heart, and the ever-moving compassion of His nature toward all men; but side by side with the bright and wondrous story of infinite pity and untiring compassion, you have the record of human failure, disobedience, rebellion, murmuring. Every dispensation—the Garden of Eden, the Period of Conscience, the Patriarchal Age, the Mosaic Economy, the Days of the Kings, the Times of the Prophets—ends in failure, and when God looks upon the people whom he had called and created, in order that they might be a blessing to the whole earth, He says to them: "Lest I come and smite the earth with a curse." But in that first word of the last clause shines a ray of hope and of gladness—"*Lest* I come."

The Old Testament does not end with a curse pronounced, but with a curse threatened, not with a word declaring that hope is forever past, and that there can be no redemption and no deliverance, no further word, but with a statement intended to teach that God has not yet pronounced this curse, and that He does not desire to do so. "Lest I come and smite the earth with a curse." The word with which the prophecy and the old dispensation end—end, that is, so far as their teaching is concerned—is the last appeal of love, and is aimed at averting calamity, by announcing it as the natural sequence of disloyalty and sin.

The Jew always understood this as a message of love, and the Rabbis in the Synagogue from then until the coming of Christ, and in the days of Christ, and until this day, never end Malachi with its last verse. They conclude with the fifth verse. Reading the last: "And He shall turn the heart of the fathers to the children; and the heart of the children to their fathers, lest I come and smite the earth with a curse;" they revert to the fifth: "Behold, I will send you Elijah, the prophet, before the coming of the great and dreadful day of the Lord."

In the Septuagint, the fourth verse is lifted out of its place and put at the end, so that the Bible does not end with the curse. Take the verses five, six, and four, and read them in sequence: "Behold, I will send you Elijah, the prophet, before the coming of the great and dreadful day of the Lord. And he shall turn the heart of the fathers to the children, and the heart of the children to their fathers, lest I come and smite the earth with a curse. Remember ye the law of Moses, my servant, which I commanded unto him in Horeb for all Israel, with the statutes and judgments." The fact that the Rabbis read the passage in this way, and that the Septuagint has lifted the fourth verse without altering the number, and put it at the end, reveals most unmistakably

the way in which the Hebrew nation understood this message.   They did not regard it as
a message of anger, but as a message of love;
not the pronouncement of a curse, but a warning against an awful calamity which might
befall them.   It is evident that they understood this final message to be a gospel, not of
wrath but of love, and there is no room for
doubt that their exposition was a correct interpretation of the meaning intended—that God,
looking at this people in their apostasy, fool-
hardiness, and impertinence, yet gave them
this last message before He sealed the prophetic book—a message not of anger but of
infinite love.

II

This final word then, being a warning, and
not a sentence, is a Gospel of Love, and is
closely connected with a declaration of the
possibility of escape from the threatened
curse, and a statement of the condition of
such escape.

In the promise of the coming of Elijah it is
said that "He shall turn the heart of the
fathers to the children, and the heart of the
children to their fathers."   That turning of
heart marks the condition upon which the
curse may be averted.   The mission of Elijah,
as here indicated, is not social, but spiritual.

It is not that he will come to bring about reconciliation in the families of the people. "The fathers" are the patriarchs Abraham, Isaac, and Israel, from whose ideals of life and state of heart these children have so sadly wandered, and the mission of Elijah shall be that of turning these wandering ones back to those ideals, and to that state of heart.

Paraphrasing the statement, getting the inner thought of it, and putting it in other words, we may say, Israel shall be in that day Israel indeed, in spirit and inward life, and not in the mere outward tokens of their ritual and service. The existing position, as we have seen, was that of an altar set up, with sacrifices laid thereon, and feasts, and fasts, and all the externals strictly observed, which marked them off as the peculiar people of God, while their heart was far away; so that of them Abraham, if he had moved into their midst, would have said, "These are not my children;" or Jacob, "These are surely not the sons of the man whom God called Israel." They had missed their way, and corrupted the covenant; but God's purpose could not be altered, and therefore if the curse threatened is not to become actual, then it will be because "their heart shall be turned back to the fathers, and the heart of the fathers to the children." When they shall go back to His

principles, and be what He intended they
should be: when the externals with which
they have been satisfied shall be nothing in
their eyes, save the outward expression of the
inner meaning of the covenant of their God
with them; then shall the curse be removed,
and showers of blessing fall from opened windows. That is the gospel of love.

And how is this to be brought about? "Behold I will send you Elijah before the coming
of the great and dreadful day of the Lord
(verse five). Elijah, another messenger, is to be
sent. The prophecy is not fulfilled; the matter is still open, one other voice is to sound,
one other message to be delivered, and that
voice will sound and that message be delivered just as the King Himself is coming.

The fulfillment of that promise, we all understand, was in the coming of John the Baptist; but because there are apparently contradictory verses concerning it, let us make a
digression to consider them.

John i. 21: "And they asked him"—that is
John the Baptist—"What then? Art thou
Elias? And he saith, I am not." Matt. xvii.
10–13: "And His disciples asked Him," that
is Jesus, "saying, Why then say the scribes
that Elias must first come? Jesus answered
and said unto them, Elias truly shall first come,
and restore all things. But I say unto you,

that Elias is come already, and they knew him
not, but have done unto him whatsoever they
listed. Likewise shall also the Son of man
suffer of them. Then the disciples understood
that He spake unto them of John the Baptist."
Here is an apparent contradiction. John says,
" I am not." Jesus says, " He is." The interpretation of Scripture is always within itself, and the solution in this case is to be found
in yet another gospel—Luke i. 16, 17. The
heavenly messenger in announcing the coming
of the Baptist, says of him : " Many of the
children of Israel shall he turn to the Lord
their God. And he shall go before Him in
the spirit and power of Elias "—mark how the
very words and thoughts of Malachi's prophecy are taken—" to turn the hearts of the
fathers to the children, and the disobedient to
the wisdom of the just ; to make ready a people prepared for the Lord." John said, " I am
not." That was John's answer to the literalness of the outlook of the people of his day.
They were in direct succession to those to
whom Malachi spoke, living in externals,
slavishly following the letter. When John
came, they said, " Art thou really Elias ? "
He replied, " I am not." It was a negative to
the literalness that had grown out of their
apostasy of heart. But the King Himself said,
" Elias is already come," and they knew He

meant John. With reference to his coming, the angel sang, " John shall come in the spirit and power of Elias," and it was in this spiritual sense that Jesus claimed John as the fulfillment of the word. John was perfectly right therefore when he corrected their literalness by saying he was not Elias ; and the King was true when He said he was Elias, that there was in him a fulfillment of the last prophecy of Malachi. This is an interesting illustration of the comprehension of the old dispensation in the new, by a spiritual interpretation of the things of God, which renders impossible that which is merely literal and external.

III

Between the time of Malachi and this coming of one in the spirit and power of Elias, four hundred years ran their course. During this period the Gospel contained in these final words was the only message to man. What was the forceful element therein ? Wherever it was a word of power, transforming lives and changing conduct, as in the cases of Simeon and Anna, and doubtless many beside, it was so, by virtue of the promise of the dawn of the day of God. To those who looked for the time of Divine interposition, and lived as in hourly expectation of it, life became a new experience, and in their character the Gospel

of Love wrought miracles of transformation
and beauty. The first three verses of chapter
four contain the words of that promise: " Behold the day cometh that shall burn as an
oven; and all the proud, yea, and all that do
wickedly, shall be stubble; and the day that
cometh shall burn them up, saith the Lord of
Hosts, that it shall leave them neither root
nor branch. But unto you that fear My name
shall the Sun of righteousness arise with healing
in His wings: and ye shall go forth, and grow
up as calves of the stall. And ye shall tread
down the wicked; for they shall be ashes under the souls of your feet in the day that I act,
saith the Lord of Hosts."

This is the great announcement, which abode
upon the heart and consciousness of this people for four hundred years. Certain it is that
they slighted it, and most probably argued
against it, and tried to prove it was not literal;
but it was the forceful element in the Gospel
of Love during that whole period. When
Jesus came, Simeon and Anna and a few wise
shepherds forming God's Elect Remnant, were
waiting for the day that should " burn as an
oven"; for the " rising of the Sun with healing in His wings."

Notice particularly here that while two
things are stated, they are in reality one:
" Behold, the day cometh that shall burn as

an oven;—but unto you that fear My name
shall the Sun of righteousness arise with healing in His wings." This is one event having
two sides to it. It may be in the matter of
time, reckoning things by human methods,
that one will precede the other, but the succession is within the unity. The great announcement is that of the Divine activity of
the future. God is leaving this people without a prophetic message for four hundred
years; but His final word is, "I am not
abandoning the earth; evil is not a triumphant
force; while they who perform evil appear to
be flourishing to-day, there is an end coming
to all these things." God will act! The day
cometh which shall burn; all against which
the plaintive protest of love has been uttered
in vain, shall be destroyed and swept away
when that day begins. "But to you that fear
My name"—the Elect Remnant—"the Sun of
righteousness shall arise with healing in His
wings."

And how will He act? As a fire of destruction to impurity and as a sweet balm of healing to those that fear His name. And this
day will be ushered in, not by any gradual
process, overcoming the evil of the age, but
by a sudden, abrupt transition. Elijah first,
with his last message, and then the King,
coming suddenly to His temple, the day break-

ing, the " Sun rising with healing in His
wings." How beautifully these things coalesce so far as the great central fact is concerned! " Behold the day cometh." " The
Sun shall rise." The same thing. " The day
cometh; the Sun shall rise." " A day shall
burn as an oven." " The Sun shall have healing in His wings." It is all one day. " A day
cometh." When will it come? " When the
Sun rises." " The day that is coming will
burn." How will it burn? The Sun shall be
the scorching heat that will burn, but the Sun
will also have healing in His wings. *It depends on the character of the men upon whom
His light falls whether they shall be burned or
healed.* It is the same day.

Look at it again yet more closely. " The
day cometh that shall burn as an oven." In
the fifteenth verse of the third chapter you
find these words, " And now we call the proud
happy; yea, they that work wickedness are
set up—*they that work wickedness are set up.*"
Now notice chapter four, verse one: " All the
proud, yea, and all that do wickedly, shall be
stubble." Do you see the change? When
that day cometh the old order of things
shall be reversed. To-day you are setting up
the wicked, calling them happy; but when
God's day breaks the proud and wicked shall
be as stubble. The "set-up" things of an

apostate age shall be stubble in the day of God; stubble when the Sun of righteousness is shining.

But how can these apparently contradictory things be the same? They can be no other than the same. How is day ever made but by the coming of the Sun, and to follow interpretation finely, it is by the *rising* of the Sun that there shall be healing. What men shall catch daybreak first? Not the men who are wicked and are to be as stubble, but the watchers on the mountains; souls who have been tired of the apostate age and have been saying, "Lord, come! come!" They first will see the break of the day, and to them its rosy tints will bring healing, "and the Sun shall rise with healing in His wings"; and, then, when He is risen in the meridians, strong with scorching heat, all things stubble shall be burned up.

We all know the different effect the sun has upon different things. There is a tree planted by the river; the running stream waters its roots, and the summer sunshine, falling upon it, makes it spring to green and beauty; and here is a field of stubble, and the same sun that touches the tree by the river into beauty, burns the stubble with its scorching rays. The same thing brings in the one case life, and in the other barrenness and waste. God's

message is, " My day is coming.   I shall act."
" Behold, the day cometh which will heal and
burn." It will heal the souls that wait for Him,
the wounded souls of the night.   It will heal
them, why ? Because they are planted by the
rivers of water, because all their springs are
in God, and to them God's Sun comes with
beauty, health, and light, and " healing in His
wings "; but to those on this side, the men of
stubble that are set up to-day, that have no
springs outside themselves, that have not found
their roots spreading out by the river's edge
to the eternal waters, the Sun shall be a
scorching heat; they shall be stubble in that
day.

So the word ends, Malachi's voice ceases.
He had described their condition, told them of
God's infinite love; and he makes this final
announcement, that God is not abandoning
them nor the world, that the day is coming
when the Sun will rise.   He declares to them
the different result produced upon two conditions of life, and then with pathos in every
tone of his voice he utters the Divine words:
" I will send you Elijah before that day to
turn your heart to the fathers, and the heart
of the fathers to the children, lest God smite
the earth with a curse."

Before considering the application of this
final message to the age in which we live, it

should be noted that the second part of the
Divine programme—second in order, though
first named as most needed by the people to
whom it was addressed, Mal. iii. 1—has not
yet been carried out. The King came and
preached " the acceptable year of the Lord."
There He closed the book. " The day of
vengeance of our God " still lies ahead. For
reasons that lie deep in the infinite wisdom of
the Eternal He still waits, and while we sometimes sigh for day, we rejoice by faith in His
" long-suffering," knowing that with Him our
weary years are not, for " one day is with the
Lord as a thousand years, and a thousand
years as one day." Yet surely His first advent did scatter fire on the earth, which is
even now at work amid all the upheaval and
collapse of human might and wisdom, prepar-
ing the way for the new day of God, at the
dawn of which the burning of the first kindled
fire shall answer the new fire revelation, and
leave of things wicked no root nor branch.

Point by point we have seen how solemn the
application of this final word of the old prophetic age is to the age in which we live. Christendom is largely astray to-day, and I hope
you notice I have been careful to differentiate
between the Church of Christ and Christendom. The Church of Jesus Christ no man
knoweth but Himself and the Father. No

man can say this or that is the Church, or that
it is here or there. The Church is a sacred
entity that He alone knows, which is loyal to
Him to-day and ever has been. Christendom,
the mixed multitude that calls itself by the
name of Christ, that says to Him, " Lord,
Lord," and yet does not the things that He
says, is sadly astray ; and yet the Divine love
is still brooding over all, and calling in words
of infinite tenderness, complaining to His own
people who are forgetful of the principles of
righteousness by which He will complete His
work in the days to come. Thank God, there
is an Elect Remnant. He has never left Himself without a witness, and, I believe, there
never were so many hearts loyal to Christ as
there are to-day—men and women desiring
that His kingdom should come to the earth,
and realizing that it must come in their own
lives and hearts ; an Elect Remnant, fearing
the Lord, hearkening to, and honoring the
voice of the Master.

How ends the word of inspiration for this
age ? Will you turn to the last word of the
New Testament ? " The grace of our Lord
Jesus Christ be with you all." The Revised
Version has an important alteration in this
passage. " The grace of our Lord Jesus Christ
be with the saints," instead of " with you all."
" With the saints." The last word of the Old

Testament is "Curse"; the last word of the
New, according to the revision, is "Saints."
And yet in the inner thought of these two
words there is an identity of meaning. The
word translated "curse" in the Old is the
word "devoted," as in the case of Achan and
his treasure "devoted" to destruction. "Lest
I smite the earth with a curse"—that is, lest I
devote it to judgment. The last word of the
New Testament describes the people of God as
"saints," separated, set apart, devoted. The
devotion in the two cases is as wide asunder as
the poles, but the inner thought is identical;
it is that of the sovereignty of God. "Lest I
smite the earth with a devotion to destruction." "The grace of our Lord Jesus Christ
be with those devoted to the will of God;"
God's sovereignty wearied by the old to be
realized by the new—Moses and Jesus. God
is behind and over all, and He asserts Himself
in the closing words of both Old and New.

It is needless for me to say I believe in ver-
bal and plenary inspiration. If we could only
read from the writing of the original manu-
scripts we should find every preposition in its
place, and the smallest words alive with infinite meaning. That is my stand with regard to this book of God, and I therefore see
tremendous force in this fact concerning the
closing words of the Testaments. What is the

last word of the New? "The grace of our
Lord Jesus Christ be with the saints." What
is grace? The law revealed. The grace of
God is that which pleases God, and in its application to us it is the unmerited favor of
God. What is the favor which is unmerited?
It is the love which, stooping to our condition,
teaches us how to obey the law, and not only
teaches us how, but energizes us for obedience.
I am so anxious that men should understand
that grace does not mean that God has put
morality on one side, or excuses anybody for
immorality or impurity. Grace means, we are
to be all that God intended us to be. It means
that Christ, by life and death, and resurrection
and living power, will bring into our lives,
poor, weak, wretched as they are, all the req-
uisite force that we may obey every word
that God has spoken in His declaration of His
requirement concerning man.

And what is the element of force in this new
Gospel of love? In the twelfth verse of the
same chapter you have the announcement,
"Behold, I come quickly, and My reward is
with Me." Just as the old covenant ended
with the voice that told of the coming of the
Lord, so does the new. I am not going to attempt to deal fully with the subject of the
coming of Jesus Christ. Let me simply say
that what is before us to-day—the next thing

—is His second advent. What was the last thing? His first coming and Pentecost. Nothing has happened since then! Write your history, total up your battles fought, and won, and lost, talk in praise of statesmen and politicians if you will—yet nothing has happened! As God watches the movements of men He counts upon the strokes of the great clock of Eternity, and the last was the birth of Christ and His work and Cross and Pentecost; and the next, "Behold I come quickly." There is nothing between. Some of us believe we are very near to the next. It cannot be very long before that voice sounds; but there will be a twofold aspect of this day of God, "The Sun rising with healing in His wings"; "A day that will burn as an oven,"—following one another, but only one event, the coming of Christ—first the Sun of righteousness with healing in His wings, and then the day that follows it, a day that burns. Our eyes are toward that event, the eyes of the world should also be toward that event. Knowingly or unknowingly, humanity waits in its suffering, sorrow, and sin, in its baptism of tears and blood,—for what? For the King. Parties are leaderless, and nations are all at unrest.

"Broken lies creation,
Shaken earth's foundation,
Anchorless each nation:
Lord, come away!"

The Kingdom is waiting for the King. Men who do not realize it are nevertheless waiting for Him. What will His coming mean? It depends upon individual character. To those who fear His name—the Sun of righteousness and healing. To the proud and all who do wickedly—fire! burning them as stubble.

That is no pessimistic outlook: it is the only optimism. To hope for the conversion of the world by the preaching of the Word of God in this dispensation, is to hope against revelation and fact. People are multiplying by the natural laws of increase, far more swiftly than converts are being made. Nay, the King is coming and that is the final message.

I end with a question and I leave the thought for answering solemnly when we are alone. Revelation xxii. 16, 17: "I Jesus have sent my angel to testify unto you these things in the Churches. I am the root and the offspring of David, and the bright and morning star." We, if we are in the Church, wait for the rising of that Star. "And the Spirit and the Bride say, Come." Can I say, "Come" to Christ's announcement that He is coming? "Behold, I come quickly"; can I say "Come, Lord Jesus"? There is no test concerning holiness of life and character equal to that. "I cannot say 'Come,'" says one: "there are ties that hold me here." Well, the sooner the earthly tie is riven the better; and the sooner in harmony with the Spirit we can say to Him "Come!" the better it will be for us and the earth. Elijah came before the coming of Jesus long ago, and the hearts of the children were turned to the fathers by thousands through his preaching, and I believe that to-day the signs of the times point to the nearness of the coming of Jesus Christ. There never was a day when the hunger for spirituality of work and definite teaching concerning the Book of God was as keen as it is to-day. Everywhere churches are crying out for definite spiritual life. What does it portend? I believe it is the latter rain; and next: the King!

That we may not be ashamed at His coming, let us walk with persistent and never-ceasing care. The externals are of secondary import, and will, of a natural sequence, fall into true place, if in the deepest recesses of our inner life we are true to Him.

To lonely, personal, solemn heart-searching would I call the whole of God's people to-day, and if the thought that rises most easily be the one expressed in the olden day by the question WHEREIN? then in very deed is the need for humbling before God most sure.

THE END